Western Star

By Stephen Vincent Benét

Prose
THE BEGINNING OF WISDOM
YOUNG PEOPLE'S PRIDE
JEAN HUGUENOT
SPANISH BAYONET
JAMES SHORE'S DAUGHTER
THE DEVIL AND DANIEL WEBSTER
THIRTEEN O'CLOCK
JOHNNY PYE AND THE FOOL-KILLER
TALES BEFORE MIDNIGHT

Poetry
FIVE MEN AND POMPEY
TIGER JOY
HEAVENS AND EARTH
JOHN BROWN'S BODY
BALLADS AND POEMS
BURNING CITY
YOUNG ADVENTURE
A BOOK OF AMERICANS
(with Rosemary Benét)
NIGHTMARE AT NOON
THEY BURNED THE BOOKS
WESTERN STAR

Libretto
THE DEVIL AND DANIEL WEBSTER

Selected Works
VOLUME ONE: POETRY
VOLUME TWO: PROSE

WESTERN STAR

Stephen Vincent Benét

FARRAR & RINEHART, INC.
New York   Toronto

In 1934, Stephen Vincent Benét planned and began a long narrative poem about the western migration of peoples and more specifically the pioneers, first as they came to America and then as they spread out through America toward the West. It was to be a long poem—of three, four, or possibly five books—longer than *John Brown's Body*. He worked on this for some years, put it aside while he wrote other things, and took it up again three years ago. As war came, he again put it aside to do his challenging war pieces; speeches, broadcasts, and various other tasks for the government. However, some six months ago, he put into shape, for possible publication, Book One of *Western Star*. It is this completed book, as he wrote and prepared it for publication, which is printed here. After his untimely death, on March 13, 1943, there were found on his desk pencilled papers, obviously notes for the continuation of *Western Star*, on top of which was a quatrain —probably one of the last he ever wrote:

> Now for my country that it still may live,
> All that I have, all that I am I'll give.
> It is not much beside the gift of the brave
> And yet accept it since tis all I have.

INVOCATION

Not for the great, not for the marvelous,
Not for the barren husbands of the gold;
Not for the arrowmakers of the soul,
Wasted with truth, the star-regarding wise;
Not even for the few
Who would not be the hunter nor the prey,
Who stood between the eater and the meat,
The wilderness saints, the guiltless, the absolved,
Born out of Time, the seekers of the balm
Where the green grass grows from the broken heart;
But for all these, the nameless, numberless
Seed of the field, the mortal wood and earth
Hewn for the clearing, trampled for the floor,
Uprooted and cast out upon the stone
From Jamestown to Benicia.
This is their song, this is their testament,
Carved to their likeness, speaking in their tongue
And branded with the iron of their star.
I say you shall remember them. I say
When night has fallen on your loneliness
And the deep wood beyond the ruined wall
Seems to step forward swiftly with the dusk,
You shall remember them. You shall not see
Water or wheat or axe-mark on the tree
And not remember them.
You shall not win without remembering them,
For they won every shadow of the moon,
All the vast shadows, and you shall not lose

Without a dark remembrance of their loss
For they lost all and none remembered them.

Hear the wind
Blow through the buffalo-grass,
Blow over wild-grape and brier.
This was frontier, and this,
And this, your house, was frontier.
There were footprints upon the hill
And men lie buried under,
Tamers of earth and rivers.
They died at the end of labor,
Forgotten is the name.

Now, in full summer, by the Eastern shore,
Between the seamark and the roads going West,
I call two oceans to remember them.
I fill the hollow darkness with their names.

Western Star

Prelude

Western Star

PRELUDE

AMERICANS are always moving on.
  It's an old Spanish custom gone astray,
A sort of English fever, I believe,
Or just a mere desire to take French leave,
I couldn't say. I couldn't really say.
But, when the whistle blows, they go away.
Sometimes there never was a whistle blown,
But they don't care, for they can blow their own
Whistles of willow-stick and rabbit-bone,
Quail-calling through the rain
A dozen tunes but only one refrain,
"We don't know where we're going, but we're on our way!"
—Bird-whistles, sleepy with Virginia night,
Veery and oriole,
Calling the morning from the Chesapeake
To rise, in pomp, with redbud at her breast,
The whistles of the great trains going west,
Lonely, at night, through cold Nebraska towns,
The chunking of the bullfrogs in the creek
Where the forgotten wampum slowly drowns,
Cow-horn and turkey-call,
And last, purest of all,
The spell of peace, the rapture of the ear,

3

The water-music mounting into light,
The hermit thrush that is New England's soul—
These are the notes they hear.

Americans, what are Americans?
I went downtown as I had done before.
I took my girl to town
To buy a calico gown,
I traded in my pelts at Offut's store.
And then, when I came back, the folks were gone,
Warm ashes on the hearth, but nothing more.
And, if you ask me just what made them go,
And what they thought they'd find by going there,
Why, you can ask the horses, or the Ford,
Hauling its gipsy children through the mud,
With the wry klaxon croaking "Going on!"
And the tame rooster on the running-board.
But I don't know—I do not really know.
I think it must be something in the blood.
Perhaps it's only something in the air.

Oh, paint your wagons with "Pike's Peak or Bust!"
Pack up the fiddle, rosin up the bow,
Vamoose, skedaddle, mosey, hit the grit!
(We pick our words, like nuggets, for the shine,
And, where they didn't fit, we make them fit,
Whittling a language out of birch and pine.)
We're off for Californ-iay,
We're off down the wild O-hi-o!
And every girl on Natchez bluff
Will cry as we go by-o!

So, when the gospel train pulls out
And God calls "All aboard!"
Will you be there with the Lord, brother,
Will you be there with the Lord?
Yes, I'll be there,
Oh, I'll be there,
I'll have crossed that rolling river in the morning!

2

The stranger finds them easy to explain
(Americans, I said Americans,)
And tells them so in public and at length.
(It's an old Roman virtue to be frank,
A tattered Grecian parchment on the shelves,
Explaining the barbarians to themselves,
A lost, Egyptian prank.)
Here is the weakness. On the other hand,
Here is what really might be called the strength.
And then he makes a list.
Sometimes he thumps the table with his fist.
Sometimes, he's very bland.
O few, stiff-collared and unhappy men
Wilting in silence, to the cultured boom
Of the trained voice in the perspiring room!
O books, O endless, minatory books!
(Explaining the barbarians to themselves)
He came and went. He liked our women's looks.
Ate lunch and said the skyscrapers were high,
And then, in state, passed by,
To the next lecture, to the desolate tryst.

Sometimes to waken, in the narrow berth
When the green curtains swayed like giant leaves
In the dry, prairie-gust,
Wake, with an aching head, and taste the dust,
The floury wheat-dust, smelling of the sheaves,
And wonder, for a second of dismay,
If there was something that one might have missed,
Between the chicken salad and the train,
Between the ladies' luncheon and the station,
Something that might explain one's explanation
—But not for long—for nothing could be missed.
(We paid him well, so nothing could be missed.
We showed him all the sewers and the cars,
We gave him a degree at Convocation.)
He talked—and all outside, the prairie-day
Drowned into evening, and the shadows spread,
And, by the muddy river, miles away,
The outcast found the Indian arrowhead.

3 .

And I have listened also, in my youth,
And more than once or twice,
To the trained speech, the excellent advice,
The clear, dramatic statement of the sum,
And, after it was dumb,
Heard, like a spook, the curious echo come,
The echo of unkempt and drawling mirth
—The lounging mirth of cracker-barrel men,
Snowed in by winter, spitting at the fire,
And telling the disreputable truth

With the sad eye that marks the perfect liar—
And, by that laughter, was set free again.

So, when you ask about Americans,
I cannot tell their motives or their plans
Or make a neat design of what they are.
I only see the fortune and the bane,
The fortune of the breakers of the earth,
The doom arisen with the western star.

Oh yes, I know, the double trails have met,
The long traverse is done, the scent is cold,
The blaze dies out upon the fallen tree.
We have another hope to make us old,
Another, and a truceless enemy,
And, of the anguish and the bitter sweat,
Nothing remains but little words. And yet—

Star in the West, fool's silver of the sky,
Desolate lamp above the mountain-pass
Where the trail falters and the oxen die,
Spiked planet on the prairie of wild grass,
Flower of frost, flower of rock and ice,
Red flower over the blood sacrifice.

There is a wilderness we walk alone
However well-companioned, and a place
Where the dry wind blows over the dry bone
And sunlight is a devil in the face,
The sandstorm and the empty water-hole
And the dead body, driven by its soul.

But not the first illusion, the new earth,
The march upon the solitary fire,

The casting of the dice of death and birth
Against a giant, for a blind desire,
The stream uncrossed, the promise still untried,
The metal sleeping in the mountainside.

That sun-dance has been blotted from the map,
Call as you will, those dancers will not come
To tear their breasts upon the bloody strap,
Mute-visaged, to the passion of a drum,
For some strange empire, nor the painted ghosts
Speak from the smoke and summon up the hosts.

And, for the star that made the torment brave,
It should exist, if it exist at all,
But as the gleam of mica in the cave
Where the long train roars like a waterfall
And the steel shoes bite down upon the steel,
A spark ground out and dying on the wheel.

Star-rocket, bursting when the dawn was grey,
Will-o'-the-wisp that led the riflemen
Westward and westward, killing down the day,
Until, at last, they had to turn again,
Burnt out like their own powder in the quest
Because there was no longer any West.

Only the treeless ocean, and the shock
Of the long roller, breaking from Japan,
The black sea-lion, roaring on his rock,
But never a quarry for a rifleman
Until the windy night came down once more
And the sea rustled like a forest-floor.

Then it arose, beyond the last dark wave,
Mockingly near, unmercifully far,
Cold with enchantment, naked from the grave,
The free-born image, the outlier's star,
The loadstone of the iron in the breast,
Never to be forgotten or possessed.

Rose, glittered like an idol, and was gone,
Leaving its battered servants to their fate,
The land fenced in, the golden apple won,
Plow, saw and engine building up a State,
And certain men, discarded from their wars,
Too long deceived to follow other stars.

Old riders in the saddle of the past,
Old sergeants, carrying Apache lead,
Old signal-smokes, grown meaningless at last,
—Why should one voice play bondsman to the dead,
Or rake the ashes of the desert fire
For any token of that lost desire?

Why should one song go nosing like a hound
After a phantom in a hunting shirt,
Or mark again the dark and bloody ground
Where the enduring got their mortal hurt,
Where the knife flickered and the arrow sung
And the Spring wind was bitter on the tongue?

If that were all, there might be little worth
In diligence or custom or the bare
Lust of the mind to plow rebellious earth
Because its metal found resistance there

9

And nothing but the granite could retain
The hard line, cut in the unwilling grain.

But, where the ragged acres still resist
And nothing but the stoneboat gets a crop,
Where the black butte stands up like a clenched fist
Against the evening, and the signboards stop,
Something remains, obscure to understand,
But living, and a genius of the land.

Something the ponies know,
The last, rough-coated ponies of the plains,
Scraping their little forefeet in the snow
All winter long to find the buried grass,
In the high uplands, out beyond Cheyenne,
Rumps turned against the blizzard, patiently
Enduring all the outrage of the sky,
Waiting like gods for Spring to come again,
While their wise eyes remember the Spring rains
And the whole mountain blossomed overnight
Into a world of green, and tiny flowers,
Something surpassing any song of ours,
Something as casual as air and light,
Something that passes—and that does not pass.
It always has been so.

4

Out of your fever and your moving on,
(Americans, Americans, Americans,)
Out of your unassuaged and restless hearts,
Out of your conquest, out of your despair,

I make my song. I call
Straitly upon the Four,
Earth, Water, Fire, and Air,
Dark earth of exile, Earth, the Indian-giver,
Sun of the desert, Water of the great river,
And Air, that blows the painted leaves of Fall.
I blow my smoke the ceremonial ways.
I say the ways are open for the ghosts,
Open for rolling wagons and strong teams,
For the slow wheels of Conestoga carts,
Creaking like fate across the prairie days,
For wolf and owl and bear
And the long hunter, secret as them all,
Fed at their tables, nourished with their meat,
And robbing each for scraps of forest-lore,
For all the moccasined feet
That whispered by the solitary streams,
Red bead and white, sachem and renegade
And the poor Jew who followed for the trade
And lost his pack of trinkets with his hair,
The bound who would be freed,
The sowers of wild seed,
The runners through the storm,
The women who gave birth
Stretched on the naked earth
With an old beaver-pelt to keep them warm,
The broken, who were broken for the tales,
The lost, the eaters of the locoweed.

I call upon the sorrow of the forest,
I name the places where the blood was shed,

And, for the hours when the need was sorest,
The brokenhearted camps of no return
Where the wood smoldered and the water stank
And the forgotten wounds began to burn
As the sick men divided the last bread,
I set the token by the riverbank,
I scatter the cornmeal for the great dead.

5

O whistlers who could carry that lost air,
Americans, who whistle as you go!
(And, where it is you do not really know,
You do not really care.)
Lend me your music for a little while,
The vagrant music of ten thousand marches,
Common as dust, the gay, forsaken lilt
Twanged on a banjo and a frying pan
That bore the footsore on for one more mile,
The song that built its own triumphal arches
Of lath and plaster on a floor of silt
And never looked behind to see them fall,
Till I can see the fate, and see it all,
With something of the wonder and the awe
Those mutinous sailors saw,
Dogs of the sea and sweepings of the dock,
When the Italian devil drove them on
Past all known land, into the utter seas,
Into the whirlpool, into nothingness,
And, after all the travail and the stress,
The mortal struggle and the mortal fear,

They tumbled up at dawn,
Sleepy and cursing, damning drink and bread,
To see before them there,
Neither the kraken nor the loadstone rock,
But, thin with distance, thin but dead ahead,
The line of unimaginable coasts.

Western Star

Book One

BOOK ONE

O F SEA and the first plantings and the men,
    And how they came in the ships, and to what end.

———————

There was a wind over England, and it blew.
(Have you heard the news of Virginia?)
A west wind blowing, the wind of a western star,
To gather men's lives like pollen and cast them forth,
Blowing in hedge and highway and seaport town,
Whirling dead leaf and living, but always blowing,
A salt wind, a sea wind, a wind from the world's end,
From the coasts that have new, wild names, from the huge
    unknown.

Gather them now, the pollen and the wheat,
The hardy sailors, staring at the new shore,
Ready to smell the spices that are not there,
The great sea-wolves that looted the pride of Spain
And riddled the Grand Armada and sunk it deep,
The men whose ships were the terriers of the sea,
Drake and Fenner and Grenville and all the rest,
Hawkins, the slaver, High Admiral of England,
Sailing his ship *The Jesus* to black-faced lands,
And Raleigh, with his fatal and gilded dream.
Gather the dedicate of the Northwest Passage,
The seekers of the false loadstone, drowned in the dark,

(It must be there. We know that it must be there.
We lost three ships out of four but it must be there.
Our Admiral believed it unto the end.)
(There was a wind over England and it blew.)
There is ice to the North and Spain has the golden mines,
But, in between, there are wonders. Have we not seen?
A fair, fresh land—yea, an earthly Paradise.
We touched at the shore. We gathered up sassafras.
And the savages came smiling with little gifts,
A gentle people and comely. We saw the pearls.
There were baskets full of the pearls in every hut.
We saw the sand of the rivers bright with gold.
Yet, being few, we departed. But next year—
For we questioned their king, a sober and stately prince,
And he swears that beyond the mountains—

                                        Gather them up.
("Have you seen the live Indian at the 'Rose and Crown'?
He drinks strong ale like a Christian and knows his name.
Nay, this is the honest Indian. The one before
Was nought but a blackamoor with a painted face
And hath since avouched it, sore to his keeper's shame.")
Gather them up, the sailors and adventurers,
Gather the credulous
Who looked for nutmeg-trees on the Kennebec
Bold-hearted children of the youth of England
And saw the Triton swimming in Casco Bay.
("Fortune my foe! 'Tis but one marvel more!
We will believe them all, believe them all!")
And with them, gather the others, the seemly men,
The merchants, trading with Muscovy and Ind,
Grave in their gowns of velvet, worshipful sirs,

And passionate as schoolgirls in their ire,
The gamblers, dicing for twenty times the stake.
("Have you heard the news from Virginia, have you heard?
I have a small adventure with the Levant,
And that should profit—but this hath a nobler sound,
Nobler and worthier and more excellent.
Oh, the fine great mountains of gold! Have you heard the
    news?
Nay, I'm not to be coney-catched with the first, wild tale
But Whittington sold his cat for a thousand pound,
As we read, and am I a lesser man than he?
Oh, hear Bow bells ring out for merchantmen,
Turn again, Whittington,
Turn again, Whittington,
Thrice Lord Mayor of London!")

Gather the other gamblers, the hungry lords,
The splendid, casual peacocks of the court,
Greedy as cuckoos, bold as kingfishers,
The men with the little beards and the reckless eyes
Who shine and go to the Tower and shine again,
Or die on the headsman's block with their hands stretched out
And a last fine phrase in the mouth.
("Have you heard the news from Virginia? Have you heard?
The Earl hath a hand in the venture—God bring him shame!
He came all huftytufty into the hall,
A very pious Aeneas in taffety,
Trussed up to discover marvels—and yet, and yet,
Getting is got by getting—we know the saw—
And the old fox would not bark without sure advice.
Were there half the gold that he talks of—nay but half

I could pull down Cullingdon Manor and build anew.
I'd have boxwood walks and gods out of Italy
And a masque with Hercules come out of a cloud
—Nay, Jason rather—there is matter in Jason—
I'll do it, though I venture two hundred pound.
Have you heard the news from Virginia?")

Gather them up, the bright and drowning stars,
And with them gather, too,
The clay, the iron, and the knotted rope,
The disinherited, the dispossessed,
The hinds of the midland, eaten by the squire's sheep,
The outcast yeoman, driven to tramp the roads,
The sturdy beggars, roving from town to town,
Workless, hopeless, harried by law and State,
The men who lived on nettles in Merry England,
The men of the blackened years
When dog's meat was a dainty in Lincolnshire,
(Have you heard the news from Virginia?)
The poor, the restless, the striving, the broken knights,
The cast-off soldiers, bitter as their own scars,
The younger sons without office or hope of land,
Glover and cooper, mercer and cordwainer,
("Have you heard the news from Virginia? Have you heard?
Wat swears he'll go, for the gold lies heaped on the ground
And Ralph, the hatter, is ready as any man.
I keep my shop but my shop doth not keep me.
Shall I give such chances the go-by and walk the roads?
I am no hind to scratch in the earth for bread.
Nay, a stocking-weaver I, and of good repute
Though lately dogged by mischances. They'll need such men.

Have you heard the news from Virginia?")
Gather the waifs of the London parishes,
The half-starved boys, the sparrows of London streets,
The ones we caught before they could cut a purse,
And bind them out and send them across the sea.
("They will live or die but at least we are rid of them.
We'll pick the likeliest ones. Boy, what's your name?
Good lad. You sail in *The Fortune*. The fool looks mazed.
Well, give him a wash and see he is fitted out.
We'll settle his master later.")
                                    Oh, spread the news,
The news of golden Virginia across the sea,
And let it sink in the hearts of the strange, plain men
Already at odds with government and church,
The men who read their Bibles late in the night,
Dissenter and nonconformist and Puritan,
Let it go to Scrooby and stop at the pesthouse there,
Let it go to the little meeting at Austerfield.
(We must worship God as we choose. We must worship God
Though King and law and bishop stand in the way.
It is far, in the North, and they will not touch us here,
Yet I hear they mean to harry the sheep of God
And His elect must be steadfast. I hear a sound
Like the first, faint roll of thunder, but it is far.
It is very far away.
Have you heard the news of Virginia?
                                    Friend, I have heard
The burning news of the elections of God,
The comfortable word, the clear promise sealed,
My heart is shaken with grace to my heart's root.
I have prayed and wrestled and drunk at the living fount

And God walks with me, guiding me with His hand.
What matter your little news and your tinsel world?)

Have you heard the news of Virginia? Have you heard
The news, the news of Virginia?

———————

Dickon Heron was turned thirteen,
Born while Elizabeth still was Queen,
Little but nimble, a sharp-nosed lad
With London in him for good or bad,
But with more of the gipsy in his looks
Than one finds in the sons of pastry cooks,
(And that went back to a bed of fern
And a moonlit night in Leicestershire,
And the black-eyed outlier, Alleyn Hern
Who poached for women as well as deer)
He'd never smelt fern in the deer-trod brake
Or heaped the cream on the saffron-cake
Or ridden the rollers, huge and hoar,
Where the sea-wind beats on the Devon shore
And the Devon men are kings of the sea,
But his mother came from Lytchingley
Where the sea-gull screams at the kittiwake
And the stones in the streets remember Drake.
—A slow, vast woman, marveling still
At her cocksparrow husband's thrusting will,
And with something left in her kindly speech
That London could neither uproot nor teach.
She'd lived in London since she was wed
But her hands still smelt of country bread.

She'd borne ten children and buried five
And Dickon, the youngest, would surely thrive,
Bound a prentice to Master Knapp,
He carried his fortune in his cap,
Or so said his father, often enough,
For a mercer dealt in steady stuff,
"And not in your cursed cates and tarts,
With sugar a price that would break men's hearts,
And when is my lord to pay the Scot
For the pounds of comfits my lady got?
I have gone to his steward and said my say
But he fubs me off from day to day,
And, as for mine host of the 'Bell and Keys',
May God requite him his villainies!
Serve him cat's meat? I would I had!
'Twas his own rank hare, and hath made him mad!
But, host and lord, they are all in a tale!
I'd as lief cry cockles in Newgate Gaol!
Wife, go fetch me a stoup of ale!"
Dickon listened with merry eyes,
And knew that he, too, must thrive and rise,
Rise as his cocksparrow father had,
For there's always luck for a London lad
And a bold cocksparrow can get his meat
When my Lord's fine hawk finds nothing to eat.
Oh, the London sights, and the London smells,
And the churches, jangling their Sunday bells!
He was lodged in a garret with Master Knapp
But he carried his fortune in his cap
And he loved the bustle and push of Chepe
Where half the world seemed fallen aheap,

With the prentices crying "What d'ye lack?"
No matter if trade were brisk or slack,
A lord's coach rumbling, two lackeys brawling,
The cat at the "Eagle" in fits and squalling,
A drunken sailor, rolling and reeling,
And, all of a sudden, a bagpipe squealing,
Where a bonnet-laird, with his tail behind him,
Went strutting the street with none to mind him,
Goose for the plucking, as like as not,
But it took rare wits to cozen a Scot!
And there, by the horns, was a black-eyed Don!
They smelt his brimstone and booed him on
While the masters muttered uneasily,
"Lads—good lads—let the fellow be!"
He passed, with his train, in black and scarlet,
While Will Payne groaned, "Oh, the Popish varlet!
What's the Spanish for son of a bitch?"
But they saw the hand on the bridle twitch,
And the cuff that his master gave Will Payne
Was cheaply bought by the shame of Spain.
Then a broadsheet-seller came crying his wares,
The Horrible Duel at Tower Stairs,
The Last Confession of Simon Oates
Who murthered his wife for a bag of groats,
News from Virginia, our golden good,
And the fine new ballad of Babes in the Wood,
With the Merry Diversions of Madcap Awdrey,
Half pure music, half naked bawdry,
And a dozen other hot-spiced delights
To vex poor prentices' dreams of nights.

Oh, the mercer's trade was a lively trade,
No backbreak business of plow and spade,
And Dickon pitied the country sheep
Who stared, big-eyed, at the noise of Chepe,
Hustled and bustled and pushed about
Till their wits and their purses were inside out,
The country cousins, smelling of cheese,
Who couldn't tell sarsenet from hodden frieze,
And yet, there were times when the sun baked hot
On stall and alley and chimneypot
Or the thin moon rode in the black Spring gales—
And then he'd remember his mother's tales,
Tales of a county of cream and curds,
The slow voice breathing the simple words,
Country living and country fare
And the fresh, salt tang in the blowing air,
"Liddle sparrow—Dickon, my own.
Sea be master of Devon men.
Mind you of that when you'm man grown,
Liddle Dickon—Dickon, my wren."
There was no county of cream and curds.
There was no reason within the words.
But they drove him down to the waterside,
Nimble-witted and gipsy-eyed,
To stare and listen and overhear
And then run home, with a tingling ear
From a shipboy's buffet, a watchman's tale
Or the dregs of a bosun's pot of ale.
And, ere he was prenticed, he'd dogged the heels
Of sailors home from a hundred keels
And heard, through the smoky tavern's roar,

The strange wave break on the stranger shore
Where the tanned men quarreled over their lies
And the crimps looked at them with codfish eyes.
They had gathered the fruits of the Isles of Spice.
They had drunk snow-water in Muscovy.
Now they warmed their buttocks and called for dice,
But, even ashore, they were still the sea,
And their sea-boots clattered through Dickon's head
Long after his body was snug in bed.
The prenticing put a stop to that.
But still, at nights, like an alley cat,
He'd slip from the garret that smelt of sweat,
Where Jack Blount snored with his forehead wet,
Out the window and down the wall
And back to the river, in spite of all.

It was perilous sport, and he knew it well,
For, at night, the devils came out of hell,
And, as soon as the blessed sun went down,
There were plenty of devils in London town
Who'd slit your gullet from ear to ear
While the watch still bawled "Nine o'clock! All's clear!"
—Midnight lurkers and bullies tried
And the rats who haunted the riverside
For drunkard's chanty or woman's squeal—
But a boy in his teens is monkey and eel
And a young cocksparrow can pick his straw
Under the noses of kite and daw,
Slip back to his garret and maze Jack Blount
With marvelous tales of his mousing-hunt,
—The lump of amber the sailor swore

Had come from a heathen idol's store,
The fight of the crews of the *Wasp* and *Rose*
And the dead man lying in Martin's Close
With his wounds all bloody and warm and new—
It put poor Jack in a clammy dew,
Till he'd look on Dick as a changeling stranger,
For Jack loved black-puddings and hated danger.

Now, though, they had had the window barred.
"I'll keep my prentices safe in ward!"
So said Gregory Knapp, alack,
With a cock of his eye at Dickon's back,
And docile Dickon, bent to his task,
Knew answers to questions he did not ask.
"No, he will not say—but the old tod knows.
I shouldn't have loitered in Martin's Close.
I scoured the bloodspots from my sleeve
But masters are sharper than we believe.
Let him bar the window. I'll find a way."
But that was harder to do than say.
Now he stood in his shirt and tried the bars.
Beyond them crowded the city stars,
Bright, and sparkling with mockery.
"Do they shine like that on the Ocean-Sea?"
He did not know—but the bars held fast
And he crouched on his pallet, beaten at last.
It was no use trying the creaking stairs
And the lock that groaned like a Don at prayers.
"Give up, Dickon—you're beaten fair!
You'll rove no more in the river-air.
But the mercer's trade is a thriving trade

And perhaps, when we have our fortune made—"
That was what fat Jack Blount would cry.
He stared at the sleeper and grinned awry.

———————

Matthew Lanyard, journeyman carpenter
In the ward of Aldgate, stared at the newborn child
Or what he could see of it for the swaddling-clothes.
'Twas a maid, they said. He was glad for a little maid
But, most of all, for his Rose, with her labor done.
All whity and peaked she looked, and her cheeks were
      thin,
Though she'd be better of it. 'Twas woman's work
But it frighted a man when it happened, na' the less.
There was nought for a man to do and they made you know
      it,
Though they were good, kind gossips, the neighbor women,
Even lusty Mother Billington, with her wen
And her hen's cackle of "Ducky, adear, adear,
Oh, the poor soul, how she shudders! Come, bear down, soul!
'Twill be worse ere it is better. Bear down, bear down!
I'll warrant you none so choice of your Matthew now
As you were when this imp was gotten—but 'tis all one—
They bear us down—tch, tch—and we bear for them,
'Tis the way of the world in pear-time. Come, shake the tree!
How pretty she cries, poor lamb!
                                          An I had my way,
'Twould be turn about with the bearing—eh, gossips, eh?
My Jack would screech like a goose, I'll warrant you,
With something in his belly beside his ale!
But, there it is—all honey they are, and cream—

28

Now there's a brave push!—but, once they have got their
    will—
Fetch the linen, gossips!—why them, they must have their
    way—
Were they served like gib-cats, I say, 'twould but serve them
    right,
And yet, it would be a pity, in the Spring."

He hadn't heard all of her skimble-skamble stuff
But he had heard Rose's cries for the last hour
And the sweat still stood on his forehead.
                        Now, with the queer
Unaccountable way that women had,
They were making light of it all and cockering Rose,
Telling her that the maid was a bouncing bet
And next time she'd have a boy. How could they do it?
And the room smelt
Queerly of birth and blood and all bearing women
And had nothing at all to do with him and Rose,
With the way they lay close at night, with the candle out,
And the pride she had in her three new pewter spoons
Bought at Bartholomew Fair.
                  He stood, big-boned,
With his wheatsheaf hair on end and his blue eyes dazed,
Gawky with youth, a father at nineteen.
He did not know that the gawkiness was touching
But the women did—except for the girl in the bed
Who had not known that her body could hold such pain.
But it was fading now, and she was glad.
She looked at him with eyes of love and trust.
Was he not strong and older and her husband?

She wasn't little Rose Allen any more
Who wept when the winter weather chapped her hands
And the night wind blew in the chimney and Sister pinched.
She was Goodwife Lanyard and she had borne a child,
Her child and Matthew's.
                              Nay, but the child was God's
And must be taught so. It could not be otherwise.
For she and Matthew were one in the new faith,
The pure, strong faith, and must show it before the world.
She had cried to the Lord and the Lord had answered her.
Yea, even in Mother Billington He had answered,
For Mother Billington had been gross but kind.
Perhaps she could reason with Mother Billington,
When she felt better, and teach her more cleanly speech,
Yea, even bring her humbly into the sheepfold
Where Pastor Henderson preached such goodly things.
But she giggled a little, weakly, thinking of that.
Mother Billington was no sheep but a tough old ewe,
She could see her butting at good Pastor Henderson.
"Cocksbody! A Puritan, I? Oh, go fish—go fish!
Nay, give me Easter at Paul's with all London there
And the great, proud organ bawling out like a boy
And a bishop to preach the sermon roundly forth.
Why, soul, 'tis as fine a sight as a Lord Mayor's Show!
As I'm fertile woman, I'll hold by Church and State.
You get no little hymn-singers out of me!"
And such thoughts were wicked—but she wasn't good at
    reasoning—
Only at loving—
                    And Matthew—
                              "Matthew," she whispered,

30

"Why doesn't he take the baby?"
                              "Adear, adear,"
Said Mother Billington, comfortably, drinking posset,
" 'Tis only a man, my bird, and what would ye have?
My Jack was so mazed with his first, he was clean struck
    dumb.
'A sat for an hour, dandling the tongs
And calling them 'Baby Jacky'.
                              Hoy, Master Lanyard,
D'ye know there's a new little Puritan in the world?
Or are ye feared of a wetting?"
                              Matthew flushed
And took the strange parcel, stiffly. It mewled a little,
Opened eyes like Rose's, shut them, and mewled again.
"Why, the little maid!" thought Matthew, "The little maid!"
While a queer stab went through his flesh. They were Rose's
    eyes
And Rose was looking at him.
                              "Well?" she whispered,
In the endless question of women.
                              "Why, Rose—" he stammered,
" 'Tis a likely maid—and it hath thy eyes, not mine—
But thou—oh, how could I hurt thee!—let us praise God
For thy safe deliverance—and, oh Rose—dear Rose—"

"Adear," said Mother Billington, with a sniff,
"There'll be less praising of God in a year or twain
When there's more noses to wipe."
                              But she took the child
And Matthew fell on his knees by the big bed,
"Dear Rose—dear Rose!" How little she looked, and spent!

31

They must pray, of course—but, with all the gossips there—
And it was still new to him, this faith of hers,
He liked the stubbornness of it and the plain speech
And a man's own fight for a man's own hand and soul,
But he'd still have been Church, if it hadn't been for Rose.
Her people would know what to do—and they'd been sum-
    moned—
But the pains had come on so piercingly quick and hard—
And now, thank God, it was over!
                              He felt a vast
Relief, and a strange, shy pride. They'd gotten a child
And the other journeymen would be gay tomorrow.
Well, let them crack their jests. He'd pay for the beer.
'Twas custom, even if Rose—dear Rose—poor Rose—
"What shall we name the maid?" he whispered now.
The grey-blue eyes opened in the thin face.
The tired hand closed and was one with his own hand.
"Humility," she said, in a voice like steel.

———————

Sir Thomas Smyth, in his house in Philpot Lane,
—The great, sage merchant with the golden hand,
Honored by kings, trading with half the world—
Sat with a map before him and stared at it.
There was a ragged coast upon the map.
True-drawn or false? 'Twas what one never knew,
Never until the men had voyaged there
And then not surely—but it haunted him
And had for nearly twenty years by now,
The old dream of Virginia, Raleigh's dream.

"And Raleigh's in the Tower and sits still,
Who used to strike a ball with kings and queens.
Fool, to fall out of favor with the King!
But he's the same, and still will be the same,
The boy Apollo, greedy as the grave,
Restless as fire, vain as a popinjay,
And hateful as the adder to his foes;
A sort of demi-dragon of the Queen's,
(She kept such) that would spit out fire and smoke,
Great plans, smart verses, idiot policies,
And all together, with such arrogance,
Such fine bravado, such mad lust for gold,
It seemed, at times, he shook the 'stablished world
And dazzled like a comet in men's eyes.
Well, comets are soon done.
                              Had he but sense,
He could have fixed himself upon the sky
Like a new constellation—and is lost
With his Guianas, in a little smoke,
The smoke of drunk tobacco, the grey ash.
Nay, I'll not weep for him—and yet, and yet,
'Twas greatly planned, the scheme at Roanoke,
Might have succeeded—'tis the chance we take—
And ended in disaster and despair
And a bankrupt patent.
                              Well, we bought it up,
The patent that he never should have had,
Thought of it, pondered, put the thing aside,
And now it stirs—years later, many years—
Breathes—aye—like something that has lain asleep.
A chrysalis we shut within a box,

33

Forgot and turned aside from—and it stirs—
And, with it, something stirs in me as well.

I have much honor. I have gotten gold.
And, would they found a company to trade
For unicorns with double-headed men,
They'd come to me for backing—I can hear them—
'Sir Thomas Smyth, liveth in Philpot Lane—
Aye, the great merchant—known in Lombardy,
In Muscovy and Ind and the Levant—'
And so they come, flies of a summer's day,
Bold captains, doughty swindlers, sharp-nosed lords,
And so I listen, since it is my trade,
Turn some aside, break some, 'stablish a few,
Build here, tear down there, make them serve my will,
And buy up bankrupt patents at a price,
For that's my trade as well—but that's not all.
The pride of it is seeing something stir
That you thought long forgotten. And it stirs.

Now, take the map. The map is what we know
And it means nothing. I've seen many maps,
Talked to a thousand seamen, in my time,
And, in the end, there is but this to say,
One ventures as one ventures.
                                        Here it is,
The ragged coast—the coast that no one knows.
How far the lands march inland?
                                        No one knows.
Is there a Northwest Passage to the East?
Is there Cathay beyond? Can Englishmen

Live there and plant and breed there?
                                        No one knows.
And yet, I know this much. It must be tried.

My one man's life hath seen this England grow
Into a giant from a stripling boy
Who fenced about him with a wooden sword
And prattled of his grandsire's wars with France
—The long, the ruinous wars that sucked us dry,
Wars of the Roses, nightmare, endless wars,
Wars with the French, and beaten at the end—
Then we turned seaward. Then the trumpets blew.
And, suddenly, after the bloodshot night
Of Mary, and the gropings in the dark,
There were new men, new ships and a new world.

And yet, how did we dare, how did we dare!
How did we dare to play such bowls with Spain?
She loomed above us like a thundercloud.
How did we dare to send our sailors out
Beyond all maps? How do we dare to seize
The commerce of barbaric Muscovy,
The unimaginable trade of Ind?
I should know well, having some part in it,
And I look backwards on it, and I see
A grave young madman in a sober dress
Who, each day, plans impossibilities
And, every evening, sees without surprise
The punctual, fresh miracle come true.
And such were all of us, under the Queen,
And, though she lodged me in the Tower once

(I wonder is it damp where Raleigh lies?)
Why, that is what might hap to any man,
And she was older, then. Had she been younger
Or I less wary, she'd have had my head.
I felt it teeter on my neck of nights,
And sometimes still, I hear the scrannel voice
'Thomas Smyth, Thomas Smyth,
By God, I'll lodge you fitly, Thomas Smyth!'
Well, she had Essex' head. I was his man.
And yet for all the heading, she made England.

She made it—but tis now the hour strikes
Whether we shall be small again or great.
O knights and lords and broken gentlemen,
Sailors most bold—I'll buy you for a farthing,
And set you broiling under Eastern suns,
Bed you with scorpions and have you flayed
By savages in woodlands thick and dark,
But I will have my will, my merchant's will,
And see we keep the commerces we've won,
Nay, spread them, spread them like a giant's net
Over waste oceans and fantastic seas
Till there is not a seaport in the world
That does not know the clinking name of England.

All for the money—yet that is not all.

The Raleighs must come first—I know the Raleighs.
The gold must lure men on—I know the gold.
That is not all.
                    If that were all and all,

Why should I dawdle here above a map,
At forty-eight, scheming for half a world?
Am I not Governor of the India Company,
Knighted, adventurer in West and East,
First merchant and prime mover of my years?
Why should I risk—and yet, I know I will.
I know it must be tried.

Now to the plans and the new charter here.
The Plymouth Company's for Sagadahoc,
But we of London look more southerly
And may be right or wrong—one cannot know.
And, sooth to say,
Charter itself's a cumbrous piece of work,
But I'll not move too rapidly at first
(I have learned that), I'll sit there, at the Council,
Be grave and stroke my chin and watch their eyes,
The reverend signior, the portly man,
One can learn much by watching a man's eyes,
And, if the first attempt succeeds—'tis well—
If not—and that is where the Raleighs fail—
There will be janglings and accusations
(Good Lord, have I not seen them in my time?)
Scapegoats and empty purses and the rest,
And then a grave man, moving quietly,
Civil at need and thrusting when he must,
Might get the matter safe in his own hands.
Yea, a laborious man, a housekeeper,
No ruffler, but a merchant in a gown
Who mends the gear the wastrel flung away.

We'll steer by that—and wait—and see—and wait—
And it will be great labor—but we'll wait.

The ships they warrant sound. As for the men,
They've a good man in Newport—a sound man—
Gosnold is staunch—I'm glad that we've a Percy—
Then there's my talking namesake, young John Smith,
Full as an egg of wild-mustachioed tales,
Hot-tempered—aye—I'll warrant quarrelsome,
And yet a man to make his mark or hang.
I care but little which if he does service.
Wingfield—related with my lord Southampton
And brings some influence—Kendall, a rogue,
But bold enough—why boggle at a rogue?
Aye, they're not badly chosen for the game.
We'll give them such instructions as we may
As, not to settle in a fever swamp,
But on some healthy island in a stream
That's deep enough for fitting anchorage,
Not too thick-wooded, either.
                                   And they'll be
Governed by a strong rule, yet Englishmen
With Englishmen their rights, not serfs or slaves,
And that is reasonable and is well
And we shall see.
                         I mean to plant, my friends,
Although, perhaps, you do not know it yet.
I mean to plant, my colleagues of the Company,
Not to spend treasure and the lives of men
In one fool's foray for a pot of gold.
I am the sea and not the shooting-star,

The vise and not the rapier. And I come,
Slowly by turn and turn unto mine ends,
Squeezing out gold where others found no gold
And building on the wrecks of ruined dreams,
Because I have the labor and the skill.
Because I saw it twenty years ago.

Now, in God's name, let them go forth to sea!"

———

Raleigh, in the Tower
Watched while the sun went down in palest gold,
An Autumn sunset, Winter coming on.
He stroked his beard and there was grey in it.
They let him write and read and talk and walk,
Play chemist and discover an elixir,
Ponder an endless History of the World.
They let him do all things, except his will.

"And now," he thought, "the ships set out again,
Kit Newport leads them on, the same Kit Newport
That brought the Spanish carrack in for me,
—Set out for the Virginia that was mine,
Goodspeed and *Susan Constant* and *Discovery*—
And here am I, a leopard in a cage,
Prisoned and tweaked at by a stuttering king
With a fool's cunning and a potboy's heart,
A sort of show for greasy citizens
Walking their wives, on Sundays.
                                        'Ay—see, see!—

39

Nay, to the left—the grizzled one in black
Taking the air by the high window there—
'Tis Raleigh—atheist Raleigh—sold his soul
To devils for a heap of heathen gold,
Cozened the Queen, conspired against the King
And left his gulls to die in far Virginia.
God keep us all! I'm glad I've seen the man.
Yes, Jacky, we will view the lions, now.'

And yet I was the man. I was the man.
Ere the dice fell against me, I was he.
And, if they find the glory and the gold,
My ghost has been before.
                              It maddens me.
I had the whole adventure in my hands,
The patent and the money and the men,
And yet they died.
                      They died at Roanoke,
Vanished as though the wood had taken them,
In some wild Irish tale.
                          The ship returned
—Delayed, of course—delayed—always delayed—
And, where there had been men, there were no men,
Only the name carved out upon the tree,
Croatan.
They called and cried but there was still no sound,
Only the wild-beast silence of the forest,
The forest that had never heard of men.

They try again. Well, let them try again.
I will not envy where I may not rule.

I have my huge Guianas waiting for me,
My maps, my plans, my gilded emperor,
Ruling the treasures of ten Mexicos,
I have my prison.
                    God, three little ships!
You'd think that even this oatcake of a king
Would give three little ships to Walter Raleigh!
Had I but half what he admits these men,
I'd pour such riches in his greedy lap
He'd swoon above them lovesick, like a girl,
The El Dorado's treasure, the pure gold.
And I will have it though I die for it.
What's dying but a kind of gilded sleep,
A rattle given to a fretful child
To keep it quiet, a poor, drowsy draught
Common to any tapster, but the last
And best refreshment of the noble mind
That has known all, endured all, suffered all
And now would quit the crosses of its flesh,
The daily spites, the yearly injuries,
The trammels of court favor and disfavor,
And ruin, and the sour smiles of kings,
For the great freedom without bound or name?

And yet, I cannot die within a cage.
'I cannot die and this unconquered.'
And that was Tamburlaine in Marlowe's play,
I would I had not thought of that.
                              A king!
A king who cannot even make a verse
But baas and blethers Scots—and keeps me here.

Roanoke, Roanoke,
Good seamen, bring me news of Roanoke.
For I was once concerned with Roanoke
And thought to be a god at Roanoke."

He sighed and turned away from the last light,
Fading into the darkness, like his fame.

———

Young Percy, eighth son of Northumberland,
Fresh-faced, dark-haired, a very younger son
Of an old, great, hotheaded, daring name,
Tempered at twenty-six in Flanders wars
And now the first of endless younger sons
To seek a phantom fortune in the West,
Though soberer than most—George Percy gazed,
A little dazed, but very courteous,
At the brisk fellow on the other stool.

Ancients and captains he had seen in Flanders,
And he was no green boy to gulp the first
Wild traveler's tale, told with a sober mouth.
He'd heard stage-players rant and noble lords
Rant also, though in different vein from theirs,
And, though he kept his counsel and his peace,
There were some trifling actions of his own—
Aye, a few 'scapes—he'd seen stout fellows slain—
Slain one himself—couched in the Flemish mud—
Taken his chance of shipwreck on the sea—
And, on the whole, not shamed the Percy name,
Or thought not so, at least.

                    But this! But this
Chimera here before him! this bold-eyed,
Talkative, bearded man of twenty-seven
Who had been everywhere, been everything,
(Or so he said) a prisoner of the Turk,
(Or so he said) beggar in Muscovy,
A paladin in Transylvania
(Or so he said), shipwrecked in twenty seas,
Lover of ladies in a dozen lands,
Who, in the midst of some preposterous tale
Would say with such serenity of eye,
Such a bland visage of pure chivalry,
"Here too I found, sir, as I've ever done,
A woman's kindly help my greatest stay
In bitterest misfortune"—that you wondered,
Wondered, believed and wondered yet again,
For, certainly, the fellow was no fool
And had an infinite knowledge of the world,
Its sleights, devices and subtilities,
Ambition huge as his self-confidence
And temper hotter than a beechwood blaze.
What was one to believe? What could one say?
The other men were men predictable
But not this arrant creature with his vast
Mountain of tales, his bright, commanding stare,
His hardy body, his fantastic mind.
("And yet, he knows the sea and men and wars
However he has known them. That is true.
That much is true. I will keep hold of that.
Though, even as he talks, my fingers slip
And I am back in Ariosto's tales.

Am I awake or dreaming? Is this voyage
A voyage at all? I knew before he talked.
But now I've nigh forgotten my own name.
I sail with a chimera to the West.")
So thought George Percy, but he said aloud,
"Nay sir—I pray you—'tis a noble tale—
Continue it—you were about to say—"

"To say?" the other man said briskly. "Aye.
When I had slain the second Turkish champion,
My sword being somewhat hacked, I rested on it
Perhaps the space a bell might toll a knell
And drank a cup of waters, while the Turks
Wailed for their slain most plaintively and loud.
Then there advanced the third—a lusty rogue,
Green-turbaned, their most skillful swordsman he,
And, as he rushed upon me—" said John Smith.

———

Dickon Heron, in Christmas Week,
Felt the winter weather redden his cheek
As he hurried along through the nipping air.
He'd gotten the parcel from Master Blair,
Pinched his serving-maid, blessed his name,
And pouched a tart from his friendly dame.
Now he must back by the shortest way
Or there'd be the devil and all to pay,
For Master Knapp, with a worried face,
Was waiting e'en now for the silver lace,
"Aye sir, patience, the boy has gone."
Dickon heard him and scudded on,

But they shouldn't have sent him by Blackwall Quay
For the three ships there looked ready for sea,
Decked with flags, and a drummer drumming
And the busy wherries going and coming.
One of them spun in a river eddy
And the fellow aboard looked green already
As he clutched for his sea-chest and swore aloud
While laughter rippled the watching crowd,
And Dickon wriggled, clutching his lace,
Past legs and rumps to a vantage-place.
Now, at last, he could really see
And the smallest ship was *Discovery*,
But where were the three of them bound—oh where?
He stared through the grey and wintry air,
Wishing he'd seen it all from the first,
For this was a venture, for best or worst.
There were fine-cloaked gentlemen on the decks
With well-starched ruffs at their lordly necks,
Longsword gallant and tarry sailor
And one who looked like an Eastcheap tailor,
Small and forlorn in his brand-new jack
With his bandy legs and his stooping back,
Trying to brave it, the poor Tomnoddy,
But with fear in every line of his body—
And there, on the poop, was a limber lad
No older than Dickon.
                    It drove him mad.
"The jackanapes with his whittle-blade!
And I rust and dust at the mercer's trade!"
He thumped his parcel against the quay.
"Well, I wish them joy of the Ocean-Sea,"

Said the bitter voice of a dockside shrew,
"And joy of their Virginias, too.
For the ship may venture and come again
But my man drowned with Gilbert's men."
But the startled screech of the river-birds,
The drum and the cheering drowned the words.

Dickon woke from his long boy's dream.
They had weighed anchor. They were downstream
And the limber lad would be seasick, soon.
But he felt like someone dropped from the moon,
And where was his parcel?
                              He gulped, aghast.
But it lay at his feet and the cords were fast
Though 'twas sorely trodden and daubed with tar
And noon would be over and Cheapside far
And Master Knapp in a passion, too.
"My ribs!" thought Dickon. "He'll baste them blue!"
But what might a whipping or two avail?
He had seen them sail. He had seen them sail.

———————

There were a hundred and forty-four, all told,
In the three small ships. You can read the names, if you like,
In various spellings. They are English names,
William Tankard, Jeremy Alicock,
Jonas Profit, the sailor, James Read, the blacksmith,
Love, the tailor, and Nicholas Scot, the drum.
One laborer is put down with a mere "Ould Edward",
Although, no doubt, they knew his name at the time,
But, looking back and remembering, it is hard
To recollect every name.

"Nay, who was the man,
The oldish fellow, soon broken, did not live long?
He spoke of his children, once—but the name, the name!
Nay, it was not one of the Cassons. Them I remember.
And was it a tertian ague that took him off
Or the flux? An honest fellow, slow in his speech,
That we called Old Edward.

                              Well, well, set him down."

—It is so they perish, the cast grains of corn,
The blown, chance pollen, lost in the wilderness—
And we have done well to remember so many names,
Crofts and Tavin and Johnson, Clovell and Dixon,
And even the four boys, come with the gentlemen,
In a voyage somewhat topheavy with gentlemen,
As John Smith found.
                          A hundred and forty-four
Men, on a five months' voyage to settle Mars.
And a hundred and five men landed on the strange shore.

A fair voyage, but two months longer than they expected.
A fair percentage of loss, for they lost no ship,
Not even the twenty-ton *Discovery*.
They sailed the long Southern course—the Canaries first
Then over to the West Indies—the trade-wind course,
The track of the Genoese, a century old.
They had gone two sides of a triangle from England,
Not the one long reach, but it was the surer way.
When they got to the isle of Mona, their water stank.
They stopped for fresh and the gentlemen went to hunt,
Glad enough to stretch their legs and wander the island.

They killed two wild boars and a speckled lizard or so.
—And Edward Brookes was touched by the hot, strange sun,
April, tropic, the sun with the lizard's tongue,
And his fat melted within him and he died,
There on the rocky, green sun-beaten isle
Where the lizard crawled and the wild bull roamed in the
    woods.
He had been alive when they landed, marched with the rest.
Now he lay dead all suddenly.
                                    And the flies
Began to find him, even as they still stared.
It does not say where they buried Edward Brookes,
Who had come for gain or adventure or recklessness,
But not to die of a heat-stroke among the lizards,
Though, being a gentleman, he is remembered.
—They are not remembered, the bodies cast overside
While the captain stands for a moment with bared head,
The common bodies, the men who were like Old Edward,
Though, by the count, there was more than one of them,
Ere they came to the Chesapeake.
                                    And yet, a good voyage,
And others would fare worse in other ships,
Bad water, crowded quarters, stinking beef,
And, at the end, the hurricane and death.
Though this voyage carried a locked Pandora's box,
Sure to make trouble, sealed orders from the Company,
Naming a council of seven to rule the colony
But not to be opened till they reached their goal.
It was the way of the East India Company
But it worked badly here—on a four months' voyage,
With fifty-five gentlemen scattered in three ships

And each one thinking himself as good as the rest.
There were plots and gossiping, wranglings and suspicions,
"Have you heard what So-and-so planneth? Nay, bend closer.
My fellow heard him roaring in the great cabin,
Swears, when he's of the Council, he'll have thy head.
But we'll pull him down from his perch."
                                        The idle, human
Gossip of hot-blooded, quarrelsome men,
Cooped up together too long through the itching weeks
When you get to hate a man for the way he walks
Or snores at night or dips his hand in the dish,
But, most of all, because you keep seeing him
And cannot help but see him, day after day,
And yet, working harm, for when land rose out of the West,
The council-to-be was already badly jangled
And Smith, accused of mutiny, under arrest.

And so, at dawn, on the twenty-sixth day of April,
Just over four months from London,
They sailed between Cape Henry and Cape Charles
And saw the broad Chesapeake, and the wished-for shore.
We shall not see it as they, for no men shall
Till the end and the ruin have come upon America,
The murmuring green forest, the huge god,
Smiling, cruel, lying at ease in the sun,
And neither smiling nor cruel, but uncaring,
The vastness where no road ran but the Indian trail
And the little clearings of man were small in the forest,
The little dirt of man soon washed away,
The riches of man white shells and opossum skins,
The scalp of a foe, the ritual of the clan,

49

Squash-vine and pumpkin-seed and the deer's sinew
And the yellow, life-giving corn.
We shall not see the birds in their multitudes,
The thundercloud of pigeons, blotting the sun,
The fish that had never struck at an iron hook,
The beaver, breeding faster than men could kill,
The green god, with the leaves at his fingertips
And a wreath of oak and maple twining his brows,
Smiling, cruel, majestic and uncaring,
As he lies beside bright waters under the sun,
Whose blood is the Spring sap and the running streams,
Whose witchery is the fever of the marsh,
Whose bounty is sun and shadow and life and death,
The huge, wild god with the deerhorns and the green leaf.
We shall not see their Americas as they saw them
And this was what they saw.
Now we must follow them, into the wood.

They landed and explored.
It was the first flood of Virginia Spring,
White with new dogwood, smelling of wild strawberries,
Warm and soft-voiced, cornflower-skied and kind.
And they were ravished with it, after the sea,
And half-forgot their toils, half-forgot the gold,
As they went poking and prying a little way
In childish wonderment.
A handful of men in hot, heavy, English gear,
With clumsy muskets, sweating but light at heart,
Staring about them, dubiously but ravished,
As a flying-squirrel leapt from a swaying branch
And a grey opossum squeaked and scuttled away.

Oh, the fair meadows, the goodly trees and tall,
The fresh streams running in silver through the woods!
'Twas a land, a land!
                        They blest themselves and were gay.
And that very evening,
As they were going back to the anchored ships,
The savages came down on them from the hills,
Creeping like bears through the grass, with bows in their
    mouths,
And the sudden arrows flew in the goodly wood,
The first ambush, the first taste of Indian war.
They stood it and fired blind musket-shots through the dusk
But Captain Archer was wounded in both hands,
A sailor named Morton hurt, and the attackers
Neither hurt, nor, it seemed, dismayed, for they bore the
    lagging
Rattle of musket-shots disdainfully,
And melted back, like spirits, into the wood.
And there were the wounded men and the evening star,
The balmy night, the strange country, the shot arrows,
And it was not a dream.
                        So they went back to their ships,
And that same night opened their Pandora's box
And saw the names of their council—
                        Christopher Newport,
Gosnold and Ratcliffe, the captains of the three ships,
John Martin, George Kendall, Edward-Maria Wingfield,
And the chimera-prisoner, John Smith.
A ticklish business, for Smith was under arrest.
They would not admit him, though they were soon to use him,
John Smiths being somewhat difficult to bind.

Let us look at them now,
The first council of Virginia, the first president,
The men who vexed the peace of the forest-god.

Not all are young men. Wingfield is forty-six
And, except for Percy, of the best blood there.
A cardinal and a queen stood at his christening,
Catholics both. He's suspected of Catholic doctrine
And the charge will be brought against him to his hurt.
He has fought in Flanders and Ireland, been a prisoner,
Known bitter chances, is to know bitterer yet,
Be deposed from his presidency, return to England
And write the angry defense of a wounded man
Against Smith and fate and the miseries of the years.
"My one contention was to avoid contention.
I never turned my face from danger once
Or hid my hands from labor. I never had
But the one squirrel roasted, gave part of that
To Mr. Ratcliffe when Mr. Ratcliffe was sick.
I never denied any man a penny-whittle.
Yet they opened my coffers and took my books of account."
You can hear the passionate self-justification
In the helter-skelter words—hear the hasty quill
Scratching the page, remembering the petty stings,
The small sharp wounds men carry to the grave.
—The ever-festering wounds of the broken men
Who did as well as they could but not well enough,
Were unlucky, spent the rest of life justifying,
Dictating to a plain daughter, a bored secretary,
And moving for a revision of the case
That the rest of the world has forgotten long ago—

You were not lucky, Edward-Maria Wingfield,
Though I have no doubt you did as well as you knew.
You took your chance—had an arrow shot through your
      beard—
Starved and suffered—but could not make ropes of sand.
Some men can—and suffer the deeper wound,
The splendor of Clive, and the pistol ending all.
But now, for a while, you'll be President of Virginia,
And Smith, who will write you down, is under guard,
And the bitter days are not yet.
                              Let us glance at the others.
Newport is forty-one. He will live ten years
And die on his ship, *The Hope*, off the coast of Java,
Sagacious and a captain to the last.
Bartholomew Gosnold is captain of the *Goodspeed*,
A daring seaman, well-tried in pioneering,
He has lived in a reed-thatched fort at Cuttyhunk
And this is his second voyage to the Americas.
Would he live, he might be a bulwark, but he will die
Within four months, at the touch of the forest-god.
The ordnance of the Fort will salute his passing.
Then the others, the quarrelsome, daring, complaining shades,
Shifting back and forth in their little factions,
Ratcliffe called Sicklemore, who will take the reins
When Wingfield drops them, be plotted against and plot,
Be hated for trying to build a governor's palace,
Return to England, come back, and be killed at last
Trying to trade with the Indians—Gabriel Archer
Who will give his name to the point called Archer's Hope
And die—and sickly John Martin, who will live
For twenty years, in spite of his sickliness,

And always bicker with councils and burgesses,
And yet survive and root himself in the land.
—There are bickering men like that, and they do live
Where others die, from the very toughness of soul
That keeps them bickering.
                              And he lives for us
In name and planting and certain terrible words
Spoken by him of Wingfield, "He reporteth
That I do slack the service in the colony
And do nought but tend my spit and oven and pot,
But he hath starved my son."
                              It is such wounds
Men carry to the grave.
                              And there will be many.

Let us turn for a moment to another figure,
Who, of all of them, shines with a clear steadfast light,
Robert Hunt, the minister of God,
So ill when they lay at the Downs that no man thought
He would live the voyage, yet living because he must,
Being God's servant, to conciliate,
Appease, soften the hearts of angry men
And show the true, calm courage of the true priest
Through the hard winter and the starving time.
He will lose the few poor books of his scant library
In Jamestown fire—aye, all but the clothes on his back,
"Yet none did ever hear him repine of his loss,"
And those who rail
At others, call him still "Good Master Hunt".
For the rest complained. He did not. They marveled at him.
And we may marvel, too, and, marveling, praise.

54

Peace to your steadfast heart, good Master Hunt,
And may the wild Virginia earth lie lightly
Upon the pure devotion of your name.

Now there was a month of peace and settlement,
A rich May month with each new day yet more fair
And the smiling, shimmering country bursting with Spring,
As they went up and down, explored the waterways,
Found oysters and strawberries and turkey-eggs,
And, everywhere, the colored clouds of the birds.
They had never seen such birds, they had never seen
A finer river, a land more delectable.
There were Indians but the Indians were friendly.
The Werowance of Paspahegh sent them a deer,
The Werowance of Rappahannock came
With his train, all goodly men, to the waterside
—An Indian dandy, playing on a reed flute,
Painted in crimson and blue, with a deer's hair crown—
Oh, the fine, wild noise of the flute and the courtly savage!
It was like a masque and a stage-play and yet true,
When he led them through the woods and showed them his
    town.
It was like a strong enchantment, a waking dream
And the drums in the forest said, "We watch, we watch.
They are white men with thundersticks but they are few."
The loops of the grapevine whispered, "They are few.
Perhaps we will fight them, perhaps we will give them corn.
It is hard to know. This is new. It is hard to know."

They settled, at last, some thirty miles upriver,
Where the flood was deep. They could moor their ships to
    the trees

Of that small peninsula, islanded at high water.
It was May fourteenth when they started to clear the ground,
Build the essential fort, the essential church,
And by then, no doubt, they thought themselves seasoned
    men.
They had lived through the voyage, survived one brush with
    Indians,
Found other Indians friendly and well-disposed,
They had tasted the fruits of the land and found them sweet
As the fair, enchanting weather that warmed their hearts,
Though the sun was hotter, now. It was with good cheer
That they got their goods ashore from the ships at last,
Stretched a sail for a church-roof between two tall trees,
Saw Wingfield elected President of the Council
And slept on the low-lying, ominous shore.

And we would all have done better—no doubt of that.
We would not have squatted down in a fever-marsh
Just as the mosquitoes bred and the heat began.
(The Pilgrims did not—and yet the Pilgrims died.)
We would have known which Indians were friendly.
(Let's hope we know as much of the Martians.)
We'd not have quarreled and wrangled—with a crew
Made of ex-soldiers, fledgling aviators,
Truckdrivers, furniture-salesmen, drugstore-clerks,
Machinists, workmen, a radio-announcer
And a sprinkling of nice clean boys from Yale or Harvard.
We'd have known the Martian birds and the Martian beasts
And how to hunt them and trap them. We'd have known
The ways of the Martian climate and all the ropes.
In fact, we would have done wonders.

They were there.
They were there and raising a fort in the smiling wilderness,
While Newport and Smith went exploring up the river
As far as the Falls of the James—and returned to hear
The news of the sudden, breath-taking attack
When only the ships' guns had saved the settlement.
One moment, they had been working, and the next
The hazel arrows had rained from the thick coverts,
The Indian yell gone up.
                    And, when it had passed,
There were seventeen of them hurt, and one boy dead,
And again the clumsy muskets had done no harm.
They had had to run for them, stored in the dry-fats,
And 'twas hard to shoot men slipping from tree to tree.
But they'd be warier now, build a palisade,
Keep closer watch. They did so with toil and sweat.
But, beyond the fort were the weeds and the long grass,
The thick, primeval cover—and enemies
Who did not stand in battalia to be butchered
But crept like the forest vines.
                    It daunted a man.
Step beyond the fort—aye, but ten paces beyond,
As Eustace Clovell, gentleman, did one day,
Unarmed, on a pleasant Sunday—they heard him running,
They heard his voice crying hoarsely out "Arm! Arm!"
But he stumbled into the fort with six arrows in him,
Died eight days later.
                    And so it was, day after day.
A man would be killed or hurt or the arrows fall
Like fierce, Spring raindrops out of the smiling sky,
But, when you fired at the forest, there was nothing.

Nevertheless, at last they had their fort,
A few thatched cabins, a sturdy palisade,
Corn sown and growing, a tiny supply of grain,
A cargo of wood and sweet-smelling sassafras
For the ships to take home to England.
                                    And when the ships sailed
At the end of June, as they must, and the last spars
Dwindled down the river, were mixed with the trees
At the curve of a river-bend, there was no more England.
And the men who watched were like men lost on the moon.

———————

"Oh, have you heard the gallant news,
New-brought across the foam
Of Captain Newport's noble cruise
Whence he hath just come home?
He brings from far Virginia
Rare tidings, it is clear.
So, masters, pass the bowl about
And merrily give ear."

The little secretary looked at the lines,
Pursing his lips. His eyes traveled farther on.
Vile verse, but it would do for the ballad-singers
And they got people talking. He cleared his throat
While the starveling poet glowered and bit his thumbs.
Aye, this was more to the matter.

"There's heaps of gold and precious stones
So easy to be found
That every man may justly say
'This is Tom Tiddler's Ground.'

And, though most cruel salvages
Like dragons guard the den,
Their petty bows and heathen shows
Shall ne'er daunt Englishmen."

The little secretary smiled in his hand.
It would draw them—aye—the gold and the precious stones.
But the "cruel salvages" might be softened a whit.
Say "painted"—aye, "the poor painted salvages".
That sounded better. He glanced at the last verse.

"So, all you brave inquiring hearts
And every gallant soul,
Rise up and cry amain with me
'Virginia is the goal!'
For there we'll cast our cares away
And there our fortunes stand
And we shall live like golden men
In fair Virginia's land!"

He winced a little, reading the doggerel,
But it would do for the groundlings—it would serve
With a dozen bawling voices to sound it out.
He pushed a half-a-dozen coins across to the poet.
"Aye—'twill do," he said, with a patronizing smile,
"With the change of a word or two. You'll hear it sung."

"An there were aught else?" said the poet, anxiously,
"I should be glad to meditate—"
                                    "Aye, aye,"
Said the secretary, "We keep you in mind, good sir."

"Now, an epic," the poet said. "I have long revolved
The matter of an epic within my mind,
As, for example, the wars and exploits of Hengist—"

"And who the devil was Hengist?" thought the secretary,
"And who the devil would care? Poor rogue, poor rogue,
With his candle face and his eyes of a hungry hound.
They are all alike, these poets—and all mad."
He coughed, dismissingly, and the poet rose,
"Aye, aye, good simpleton, we will keep you in mind!"
And a pox upon all such men! Still, they'd bought the verses.
He hurried off to the pothouse to spend his fee,
Devising a Latin satire on secretaries,
Their birth, lewd habits, and final abode in Hell.

The little secretary, left behind,
Still played at busyness, but his thoughts roved,
As the thoughts of office-men will toward the end of day.
They must have a prose relation to match the ballads,
Soberer stuff but written to the same end,
Something to open purses. It helped. It helped.
It was all part of the business, the sober part,
Though mad adventurers counted it little worth.
"And yet, they have our money—play ducks and drakes
     with it
And little reck how toilsomely it is got."
Now, had they only found gold, but a little gold.
Three months should be time enough.
Yet one could not blame Captain Newport—an honest man
And left them all in good trim, having built their fort.
He could see the neat, well-ordered colony,

Buzzing and active as a hive of bees,
The gleaming river, the wild, sweet-smelling shores.
Aye, a rough life, somewhat rougher than sitting here,
And the town, no doubt, not quite like an English town,
But healthy—had not Newport a healthy look?
And think of the reward!

                    Nay, one must be fair,
For Newport had spoken grimly of the savages.
But they were naked fellows with stone-tipped arrows.
How could they hinder us long?

                    Nay, we here in London
Have the sore and drudging part of the toil.

                         God's word!
They little know how we labor on their behalf,
Devising schemes for their profit and future good.
We mean to send them silkworms and gold-refiners,
Glassmakers, too—we search for Germans and Poles
Skillful in the mechanic arts to send them,
Expecting naught in return but the simple gold
Which must be there for their taking—aye, do not ask
That the passage to the South Seas shall be found this year.
It may take two years ere they find it and we are patient.
Though, now they have built their town, 'tis but just and
    right
They should get some few rewards for the Company
And the honest folk who have backed them.

                      He sighed and mused,
Marking a line in the verses with his pen,
"There's heaps of gold and precious stones
So easy to be found—"
Poor, tawdry verse—he should know it, having paid for it,

And the hungry fellow who wrote it knew no more
Of "fair Virginia's land" then he knew of Persia.
And yet—and yet—it was lame, but it had a ring—
Buzzed in the ear—and the life would be rough and hard
But less so, now—there'd be noblemen who would go—
And a man of accounts—a trusty secretary—

For a moment, the secretary wondered and dreamed.

————————

At Jamestown, the lost men neither wondered nor dreamed.
They were dying.
                  It was the stroke of the forest-god,
Sleepily vexed at last and pointing at them
The flame-tipped arrow of the August sun,
Weaving them round with vapors from the marsh,
Coming upon them in a cloud of small
Innumerable, buzzing, deadly wings,
In the river-slime, in the mud of the steaming river.
And they die and die, and Percy writes it down,
Soberly, briefly, giving name and date,
A young, brave man, but shaken to the heart.

The sixth of August
There died John Asbie, of the bloody flux.
The ninth day died George Flower, of the swelling.

(It is hot. We did not know it could be so hot.
We did not know that the warm and pleasant sun
Could parch us so. We are thirsty and we drink.
We drink of the river-water at low tide.)

The tenth day, there died William Brewster, gentleman,
Of a wound, and was buried on the eleventh day.

(The ships are gone. There was biscuit aboard the ships
And a little, comforting store of beer and wine.
Now we live on a pint a day of wormy grain.
We watch every three nights, lying on the bare ground.)

The fourteenth day, Jeremy Alicock, Ancient,
Died of a wound.
The same day, Francis Midwinter and Edward Morrish
Died suddenly.

(Edward Morrish, the corporal.
A hardy man—had served in the Low Countries.
I saw him at ten o'clock and his face looked white,
Under the tan. He said that his belly griped him.
And at five o'clock he was dead.
Francis Midwinter he shared my watch with me.
It will pass—aye, 'tis but the Summer and the heat.
But the arrows fly from the wood and no man knows.
No man has seen the enemy in the wood.
They hide in the grass like serpents and strike like asps.
It will pass. It is sure to pass. Master Hunt has prayed.)

The fifteenth day, died Edward Browne and Stephen Gal-
    thorpe,
The sixteenth day there died Thomas Given, gentleman.
The seventeenth day, Thomas Mounslie.

(We die, we die!
There are seven dead in four days—and every morning

We drag them out of their cabins like stiffened dogs
To lie in the hateful earth of this wilderness
Where we thought to find the gold. We are sick and weak,
Burning with fever, purging out our entrails
And once we were gentlemen and adventurers,
We were carpenters and bricklayers with a trade
In kindly England—oh, the English sky,
The grey, sweet Spring, the cuckoo singing aloud!
Not these wild, bright birds, this killing and brazen sun!
And no relief but the huge, black thundercloud
That lights trees of fire in the swollen, purple sky
Over the sluggish river, but brings no sweet
Blest coolness after it, only a thicker heat,
A wearier aching.)

The eighteenth day, there died Robert Pennington
And John Martin, gentlemen. The nineteenth day,
There died Drew Pickhouse, gentleman.
The two and twentieth day of August, there died
Captain Bartholomew Gosnold, one of the Council,
And was honorably buried.

(Aye, and we fired
Volleys of ordnance and of musket-shot
For the strong man gone. And I say that we did well.
But what of the Council that he left behind?
What of our noble, Popish President?
Can they not see that we die? What is it they do?
They have the pots and the spits and the high titles,
They keep poor fellows awatch through the fever damps.
But what do they do? By God, they are all ajar.

They have set down Captain Kendall from his place,
A brawling fellow, but is he worse than the rest?
I hear that they live most fatly on secret stores,
Aye, they must have food, being councilors, and we
Starve and suffer and go to the shallow graves.
By God, are they paid by the Company to starve us?
I will lift no hand to aid them. Nay, I am sped.
I will creep to my rotten tent and perish there.)

The four and twentieth day died Edward Harington
And George Walker and were buried the same day.
The six and twentieth day died Kenelm Throckmorton.
The seven and twentieth day died William Roods.

(Toll them out like bells,
The names of the lost, the nightmare peal of death,
The price of blood for the fair, sweet-smelling land.
The small store of rotten grain is nigh at an end,
The leaders are ill and wrangling, the skull-bones show
Through the dry, pinched faces of the once-hardy men,
The men who barely shoulder their muskets now,
Who are too weak to get up from their own dung
As they lie dying in the filthy cabins.
Toll the bell, forest-god.
The brazen bell of the unbearable sky,
For the fish are leaving the river, the grain is spent.
Yet a little while and the forest will come again.
Yet a little while and there will be no town.
The green vine will grow through the logs of the ruined
    church.

The possum roll on the drill-ground, with his children.
In a little while—a green while—a forest while.)

The fourth day of September died Thomas Jacob, the
    sergeant.
The fifth day, died Benjamin Beast.
There were never Englishmen left in a foreign country
In such misery as we.
If there were conscience in men, it would bleed their hearts
To hear the pitiful outcries of our sick men.

(Water, my lads! Will no man bring me water?
Will no man come? I thought we all were friends.
Good lads, you'll not desert me in this den?
Nay, but I am not dead yet, though I ail
And cannot keep my watch. Go, tell the ancient,
I cannot keep my watch. There's water here
But, when I reach for it, it flees away,
Like the damned gold we came so far to find,
And there was something that I wish to say
If I could think of it. 'Tis hard to think,
And I am back upon the tossing ship
Or seeing the dead face of Edward Brookes,
Suddenly stricken on that rocky isle
Where we went hunting. Nay, do not grin at me,
With that chopfallen mouth of blank surprise!
We all die. Did you not know we all die?
Why, then you're no Virginia man, my lad,
Not to know that.
                Nay, nay, it is not true
I harmed the wench, and those who say it lie,

Lie in their throats most foully—nor was I
The one who stabbed the sutler. It hath done
Much injury to my name. That I avouch.
But I was born a gentleman.
                              O Christ,
Sweet Christ, a little water for my thirst!
I will give gold for water. See my gold,
Yellow as buttercups in Leicestershire
In the sweet Spring—I'll ride the pony home
For Brother is afraid of it and cries—
Nay, uncle, I repent me my misdeeds
And will amend. I swear I will amend,
Although the wench was eagerer than I,
But do not leave me here, tied down and bound
Upon this narrow bed of burning gold
With not one drop of water for my lips
And the thick tide of fever—
                              Ale, I say!
Call Billy Tapster that he bring us ale,
And we will revel till the night's worn out
And bright day pales the candle—
                              Nay, bend closer!
I tell you, I was born in Leicestershire
And my name is—it was—it matters not.
But, when you go there, tell them how I died,
Lonely and desolate in a far land.)

And it was mid-September and no hope,
For half of them were dead, and the living gaunt
Life-sickened shadows, dragging weary limbs
Mechanically to the rotten bulwarks,

Staring into the forest with dull eyes,
Knowing they had to watch for something there
But half-forgetting what.
                                  There was no rule,
They would not listen to Wingfield any more,
Kendall had been deposed and plotted escape,
Gosnold was dead, Smith newly risen from fever,
And it was the end.
                            And then, no man knows why,
There came the savages, smiling, bringing corn.

Corngivers, why do you give
That these men live?
They think that you are devils of the wood
And you have fought them once and will again,
Yet, in their last extremity, you come
As if in answer to some forest drum
To bring the bounty never understood,
To bring the food that saves the starving men.

Gods? You have seen them die like truculent fools
Where any one of you would live and thrive
And, if they have the iron and the tools,
The powder and the shot,
These things avail them not.
Their magic cannot keep their best alive.

Pity? Why should you pity them or care?
They will be greedy, soon, when they are fed.
Look in their eyes and see
The felling of the tree,
The great vine-twisted tree of Powhatan.

Look in their eyes and see the hungry man
Moving with ax and fire upon the wood,
Spoiling the rivers, digging up the dead.
This is your own destruction that you bear
In venison and corn
And the red Autumn leaf
That falls before the snow,
This is the doom of werowance and chief.
This is the breaking of the hazel-bow.

And yet, before it happens, and the great
Passionate drum of wrong begins to sound,
Ere the dead lie upon the bloody ground
And the chief's sons lie drunken in the street,
Let us remember how this happened, too,
And how the food was given, not in hate,
Liking or dazzled wonder, but, it seems,
As if compelled by something past all plans,
Some old, barbaric courtesy of man's,
Wild as his heart, red as his hunter's dreams,
—And for no cause the white men ever knew.

————

And it will happen again, on another coast,
The same gift, the same bounty, when Squanto comes
To tread the eels from the mud for the hungry men
And show them how to plant corn.
                                    It will happen so
And, had it not, the white men would not have lived,
Though they were to forget it, after.
                                    It is not quite
The picture we see in childhood, in the books,

69

Where the treacherous redskins always bite the dust,
Or appear as posed and loquacious Noble Savages.
They were neither yelling demon nor Noble Savage.
They were a people.
                              A people not yet fused,
Made one into a whole nation, but beginning,
As the Gauls began, or the Britons that Caesar found,
As the Greeks began in their time.
                                        And with the same
Honor in raid and fight and the petty wars,
The wars of hunters and tribes and little chiefs,
—Lost Iliads of the forest—and they lived
As the hunter lives, by the game-trail and the scent,
The moon's clock, the tides' clock, the clock of the great sea-
    sons,
Close to starvation always in a bad year,
Without wheel or iron or distaff, cattle or cart,
But always the sky, the forest, the corn, the fire,
The log-village that hunters can leave behind,
The tent of skins that is struck and set up again,
And always the hunting-ground,
The untamed thing, the sayings from dim past
Murmuring like leaves in the wind of Spring,
"These things are good. These are bad. You are called the
    men.
There is magic all around you but you are men.
You are here to live. You are here to be of the clan,
Perform the ceremonies, kill the deer,
Laugh and desire and fight and not forget
The sky, the earth, the sacredness, the deep bond."
—The green words said to man half-naked still,

To man, before the stone walls and the cutting iron.—
And that makes them innocent children, which they were not.
They were a people, beginning—
                              With beliefs,
Ornament, language, fables, love of children
(You will find that spoken of in all the books.)
And a scheme of life that worked.
                              We shall never know
What would have come of that scheme in the turn of time,
What cities or what nations or what fame.
But we do know this. There were men from the very first,
White men, who liked it better than their own,
And not all of them Simon Girtys—nor were all
The rescued women captives entirely pleased.
There were some who stayed in the lodges of their own will.
Perhaps they were wayward ladies, but one wonders.
It seems a criticism, now and again.
And the bitter tale,
The bitter tale in the mouths of the broken chiefs,
Put down in the white man's words but bitter still,
Bitter as the sumach-berries of Death.
Powhatan, sleepily murmuring, in his age,
"I have seen all the death of all my people thrice.
It is better to eat good meat, lie well, sleep quietly,
Laugh and be merry with you, have copper and hatchets,
Than be forced to fly from all and lie cold in the woods,
Hunted by you."
King Philip, crying out, from a bitter heart,
"I am determined not to live
Until I have no country."
Canonchet, when they told him that he must die,

"I like it well. I shall die ere my heart is soft
Or I have said words unworthy of myself."

Hear the words,
For now the long wrong begins and the long wars,
And they were men, not demons, that we broke
For the good land and the sweet waters and the corn.

———————

And now, to Jamestown,
The wildfowl came, and the first cool days of Fall,
And John Smith went exploring.
He is one of the first Americans we know,
And we can claim him, though not by the bond of birth,
For we've always bred chimeras.
                        And he was one,
This bushy-bearded, high-foreheaded, trusting man
Who could turn his hand to anything at a pinch,
Bragging, canny, impatient, durable
And fallen in love with the country at first sight.
For that is something which happens or does not.
It did to him.
                        You can see the difference in Percy,
Who is always the Englishman among the natives,
And never sheds his skin or his English ways,
A good man, an excellent colonial-governor
But not this skin-changing stepchild of Ulysses,
On fire, yes, fed or fasting, to see new things,
Explore, map out, taste, venture, enjoy, astound
And look, look, look with a fly's remembering eye,
A child's delight in marvels, a liar's gorgeousness,

And the patient, accurate pen that mapped two great coasts.
This is how they roast corn.
                              This is how their women are painted.
These are the birds, the beasts—oh, look and see!
This is a beast that they call aroughcan,
Much like a badger but useth to live in trees,
This is their beaver, big as a water-dog,
This is the toadfish, swelling in the air,
And here I did—oh, the marvelous things I did!
But the maps that I draw are true, and when I see
Without myself in the picture, I see and know.
This is their language. I will write it down.
"Kekaten pokahuntas—" and the rest,
"Bid Pocahontas bring hither two little baskets
And I will give her white beads to make her a chain."
And, in between, I will get men working again,
Shame the lazy, master the sulky, heave
My shoulder to the sticking wheel of Jamestown
And make it groan and turn till it grinds the corn.
And didn't I do it well? There is no one like me!

No, my chimera—and yet, we'll see you again,
In many shapes, before the long tale is told,
The braggarts who, somehow, carried out the brag,
The stepchildren of Ulysses, many-deviced,
"And it was proved to his face that he begged in Ireland
Like a rogue without a license," says Wingfield angrily.
Well, perhaps he did. I wouldn't doubt it at all.
For such things occur to chimeras—and if he did,
The people he begged from got their money's worth
And goggled, hearing the tale, as we goggle yet.

For this man was always alive to his fingertips.
He would not lie down and die and he will not still.
There were tears on the faces of the men sick for home?
Good God, how could men behave so, in a new world,
With a bay to explore, an aroughcan to see,
An Indian king or a possum to talk about?
How could one weep for the Christmases of England
When we never feasted more or had better fare
Than in the dry smoky houses of Kecoughtan?
How could men be sick at heart,
With a savage chief to visit and beguile,
Or a wild child-princess, bursting out of the woods,
Her train of girls behind her, shouting and screaming,
With deerhorns set on their foreheads—a Bacchant rout,
Led by the nonpareil, the daring child,
Who was to die a Christian and a lady
And leave her slight bones in the English earth
And her son's sons to know Virginia still,
Such being the fate.
                                And they were to meet again,
Years later, in England, the lady Rebecca Rolfe
And Captain Smith—a strange meeting—strange and sad,
The Indian princess in her fine English clothes
And the bearded, baldish Ulysses, both nine years older
And one very soon to die as caged things will
Just when they seem acclimated to the cage.
When he came to see her, she turned away her face,
Would not talk for hours, talked a little at last
In her new-learned English. He must still call her "child".
She would always call him "father" and be his countryman.
"And always they did tell us that you were dead.

But your countrymen will lie much."
                                    You hear the words
Evenly spoken, without bitterness,
Mere fact she had learned with other white men's facts.
But there is a bitter sadness about that meeting
And Ulysses, for once, said little.
                                    He had advised
Sagely and humbly, writing to the Queen,
That the little princess be royally entertained,
For she had a great spirit and could move her people.
Well, it had been done—and there was his nonpareil
—The red-winged blackbird of Virginia's woods
—The young, wild child—
                                    There was his nonpareil
In her fine clothes, coughing.
"Bid Pocahontas bring hither two little baskets
And I will give her white beads to make her a chain."
He left the room and never saw her again.
He was outward bound—to chart the New England coast
From Cape Cod to Penobscot.
Two thousand miles of it in an open boat.
And so, by incredible labors, make the map
That drew men's minds to New England—the laborious
Chimera, who could not look at the land and lie,
Only about himself and other men,
Who doubted gentlemen's hearts but never the goal
And, in the end, could say with a flat claim
Superbly boastful and precisely just,
"These colonies being, in some sort, my children."
He had none out of his body, for all the tales.
He had no fortune out of the lands he mapped,

Not even a twelve-pound knighthood—but they came,
Gorged on his books, believing truth and lies,
They settled Massachusetts and Virginia,
And where they settled, he had been before.

You can see why he maddened others and does so still.
But, spent and old, he believed to his last breath
That this was a good country.
We have had others since, and born in the land,
Who blessed it only while they could milk it dry
And, that being done with, cursed it in the street,
Though they were not at Jamestown or the wars
But lived more easily than men at Jamestown,
In fact, lived very well.
                              I may be wrong.
But, thinking of some well-dressed gentlemen
And well-fed ladies I have met at times
Who spent their years despairing of the Republic
And trying ways to beat an income-tax,
I think I can hear the comment of Captain Smith
Clear from St. Sepulchre's, the biting voice,
The huge chimera-scorn.

———

Meanwhile, in England, time and the world wagged on,
Ticking the intricate tune of the million lives,
The famous, the mean, the simple, the great, the cursed,
The few that we know, the many we do not know,
Whirring and turning, the wheels of the clock of time,
That turns men's lives and spins them and weaves them out,
Not to their expectations but to its will.

Tick-tock,
Tick-tock,
Cross the seas or stay,
Men will live and women bear
And time will pass away.
Tick-tock,
Tick-tock,
Plant the tree or die,
We will hear the tale of it,
Hear it bye and bye.
Plant it if you can, then,
Plant it with a will,
Every root and every shoot
Must be England's still.
Tick-tock.

June 1608—and Newport is back with news
From his second voyage—news of losses and still no gold,
Kendall shot for treason, Wingfield deposed, John Smith
Saved from a hanging by Newport's lucky arrival.
No—not the best news—and the land seems not so healthy
As it did when we discoursed of the place at first.
But he has landed a hundred and twenty men
Including six bold tailors and a perfumer.
He has seen Powhatan and the monarch seems well-disposed.
But the venturers must dig in their pockets anew.
—And a woman in Leicestershire weeps for her bad son,
Knowing the ill but remembering the child.
And Sir Thomas Smyth bides his time, and Raleigh paces
The four walls of his prison, up and down.
It has been a good year for England, a thriving year.

Though not, perhaps, for certain small, humble folk,
Farmers, yeomen, farm servants, who till the dull
Bleak fields where Nottinghamshire and Yorkshire meet,
The husbandmen of two pinpoint villages
Where the slow days pass like gray wethers.

                                        Take a pencil
And dot the map of some Middle-Western State
Until you strike upon any one-street town,
Just big enough to have a name of its own,
West Center or Pottersburg or Little Prairie
(Three blocks of street and a post office—then the fields,
And the local stops for water there, once a day,
But the main-line buses never heard of the place.)
It isn't exact but it gives you an idea,
For Scrooby was a halt on the Great North Road
(And how many post offices are there, let's say, in Kansas?
How many one-street towns?)
A pinpoint place where a handful of farmers met
With William Brewster, the educated postmaster,
To listen to Pastor Robinson preach the Word,
The new pure Word that the bishops did not know.
(And how many little churches and congregations
Will you find all over this country? How many small
Minority sects that argue and pass away?)
But, this year,
The small band made its decision. They had been jeered
    at,
By their country neighbors in the country way,
—"Puritan, 'ee? I'll give 'ee Puritan!"—
Suspected of this and that, their leaders fined
For nonconformance. Now they would flee away.

They tried to do so in secret—smuggle themselves
And their few goods out of England—and were caught,
Jailed a space for breaking the customs-laws
And then released. It wasn't harsh, for the time,
But to them it was persecution with fire and sword
And deepened their resolve. The next time went better.
One group was caught and questioned, released again,
But, at last, the whole band was safely across the Channel,
Soberly walking the streets of Amsterdam
And leaving some puzzled customs-officials behind
And a magistrate or two, who dimly remembered
A group of country bumpkins, given to praying,
Who'd been arrested on a technical charge
And then set free for lack of a clear-cut rule.
—The sort of case that bothers a magistrate,
Though part of the day's work—

                                        Except for that,
Their passing leaves no ripple behind in England.

Oh yes, it's been a good year—a prosperous year,
Dickon Heron has grown an inch in it,
The little secretary is sleek and smooth,
They like his work at the Company. The poet
Has almost completed a five-act tragedy
That will be sold for wastepaper at his death,
But he does not know it. The Earl of Northumberland
Speaks gravely of his brother in the Virginias.
"Aye, George. Would you hear his letter? 'Tis worth the
    pains.
Writ modest but shows good mettle. We're pleased with
    George."

But the Dowager Countess thinks, "Would God he were
        home!
He had six good shirts when he sailed, for I saw them made,
But he does not write how they served him, nor of his cough,
Though much about Indians. Is he thin, I wonder?
'Twould break my heart if he married an Indian girl
And I am a foolish woman to think of that.
Thank God he is living! Would to God he were home!"
Yes, it's been a good year for most,
Though not for Matthew Lanyard, carpenter
In the Aldgate Ward. He stares at a dead girl's face.
She is white and small in the bed where they lay together
And his dead son lies in her arms. She cannot be Rose
For Rose was alive and loved him.
                                    But she lies there.

Tick-tock,
Tick-tock,
Carpenter and tailor,
Tick-tock,
Tick-tock,
Venturer and sailor,
Listen to the hours strike,
Listen to Bow bells,
There are riches oversea,
Land and riches oversea,
And a witch is oversea
Weaving subtle spells.
Tick-tock,
Tick-tock,
Many men have died.

Many men will die again,
Try again, die again,
Yet the bold will vie again
For the witch's promises,
Promises, promises,
Gold and silver promises
Wrapped in adder's hide.
Tick-tock.

September 1608—and the Second Supply,
And we're getting up in the world. There are seventy-odd,
Including eight Poles and Germans, sent across
As skilled in glass and potash and other arts.
They are to make trouble and desert to the Indians
And all the glass they made you could put in your hat
But we won't know that for a while. We are getting on,
For one man brings his wife and her serving-maid.
—And the first white wedding held on Virginia ground
Will marry no courtly dame to a cavalier
But Anne Burras, lady's maid, to John Laydon, laborer,
After some six weeks' courtship—a Fall wedding
When the leaves were turning red and the wild air sweet,
And we know no more than that but it sticks in the mind,
For they were serving-maid and laboring man
And yet, while they lived (and they had not long to live),
They were half of the first families in Virginia.
Well, where do you start, when you start counting F.F.V.s?

1609—and Champlain is at Quebec,
The iron tiger who is to found New France,
He starves in a crude log hut with seven companions,

The rest died in the Winter and the fierce cold.
1609—and Hendrik Hudson sails
In his blunt *Half Moon*, for Dutch masters, to seek once more
The ever-fatal loadstone, the Northwest Passage,
And to find, instead, Hudson's River and Hudson's Bay.
(They are coming now, like bees to the clover-field,
They are coming to starve, to freeze,
To heap black curses on sit-by-the-fires at home,
To die without hope, to live
In the names of wide, strange waters and log-hut towns.
They are coming now and you will not stop them coming
With the frozen ice or the roarings of the great waters,
The blind white pestilence, walking abroad at noon,
The arrow at midnight or the lightning-stroke.
They are coming now, all death will not stop them coming.)
And, in London, the golden knight, Sir Thomas Smyth,
Sees, at last, the cards in his hands. He is treasurer
Of the new Company, under a new charter,
And busily flies the secretary's pen.
Sir Edwin Sandys is deeply meshed in the scheme,
Lord Delaware will govern the colony,
Good names—fine names—and money, money we need,
Money we'll have, money we'll conjure forth,
Broadside and pamphlet telling the gilded news,
In terms that a borax-mine promoter would envy,
Subscribe—subscribe—'tis a fortune you will get back!
Subscribe—be rich in Virginia—put down your name.
They blow and blow and the gilded bubble swells,
For this will be no chance venture of a few souls
Randomly set adrift in a wilderness,
Nay—an armada—nine ships—hundreds of men—

The greatest sea-adventure that England's known
And led by a noble lord—ah, subscribe, subscribe!

It comes to the ears of a carpenter, Matthew Lanyard,
But he hardly hears. Such things are for gentlefolk
Or idle runagates like the Billingtons,
But he is under the wrath and afflictions of God.
Why did Rose die, else?
                              How else could she have died?
There are new-cut, trenching lines in his boyish face
As he thinks it slowly out, while the big, quick hands
Get through with the work—and the day—and still no Rose—
Still no Rose—but the face of the little maid,
Biddable, quiet, waiting for him at home
And moving him with a deep and painful love.
His child and Rose's child. He must make her safe.
He cannot leave her to grow like the Billington brats,
Screaming in gutters, dancing above hell-fire.
It is hard for a man to wrestle in nightly prayer
But it must be done.
                              And there is Rose's sister,
Dark-eyed, dark-haired. She is kind. She is not like Rose.
Not like Rose, but her sister, and with the faith.
Must I lie with another woman, while my wife lies
In the grave not one year dead, not one year cold,
Must I hear another woman's breathing at night?
But it was not that—it was for Rose and the maid—
And Katharine an older sister, after all,
Yes, a good and fearful woman, modest and pure,
Sharp-tongued, at times, and with something behind her eyes
That strangely looked for a moment and hid again,

Smoky and self-consuming, a stifled flame.
And, at times, he would think almost that she hated him
In spite of her wise counsel and careful hand
And yet her dark faith was trusty. She would burn
For that faith, he thought, and stare at the flames with love.
—O window, opening into Jerusalem,
Pure, spotless city of the ransomed saints,
Where the long toil is done and the clear bird sings,
Heart-shaking joy forever,
Where the white lamb, Christ, lies down in the pastures green,
Receive the innocent, receive my Rose
And bring me to her when my toil is done,
For you are all the comfort that I have,
You and the quiet of the little maid,
And yet I must devise to live awhile,
I, sinful man.
For it is a great charge to be elect
And a great duty, and a piercing thing—

Mother Billington watched him down the street
With the child's small hand in his. "Adear," she thought,
"Who ever dreamt there'd be such change in the man?
And a proper man 'tis, too, and a rising workman,
Poor soul, poor soul—and now there's the tall puss-sister
And I smell another wedding in Aldgate Ward
But there'll be no jollity this time—nay, come up!
No stealing of bride's garters with Miss Precise
But sour beer and long prayers and a cold bed,
And yet has a smoky eye, if I know the flesh,
More smoky than she wots of. Well, it may serve,
And 'tis time, in truth, the little maid had a mother

But I'd as lief bed a hornet were I a man."
She sighed and turned to her own untidy brood.
Young Jacky had been married a fortnight now
And the girl was the breeding sort, if she knew the signs,
So soon enough there'd be grandchildren to nurse.
"When 'tis cherry ripe," she hummed, "there'll be cherry pie
And the bold young rogue had ever a taking way.
I'll warrant he gives her but little rest, of nights.
Aye, Tib—there'll be herring for supper—blow your nose!"
And, thinking of the vast
Untidy, excellent principle of life
And her young Jacky with his round-faced chit
She chuckled slowly and her heart felt warm.

Dickon Heron's heart was bursting his ribs.
He had talked with one of the men who were to sail
And a knight, no less. It was too good to be true,
Though Master Knapp had grumbled about the cloak-lining.
"Aye, Sir Gilbert Hay—but who is Sir Gilbert Hay?
These farthing knights with long swords and empty pockets!
Well, take him the stuff—but see that you get the price
And no clipped money, neither!"
                                He had the price
But that was not the dazing thing. It seemed the knight
Had marked him down in the shop for a stirring youth
And, being bound for Virginia, much deplored
That such lads must rust in London, when all men knew
The golden prizes waiting in the new land
For those with spirit. But there, 'twas none of his care.
Though, oddly enough, he had need of a trusty boy,
"Having pensioned my former fellow, a tried, good servant

And saved my life more than once in the bogs of Ireland,
But, if truth be told, too old for this sort of work,
Though he begged to go."
                    Perhaps Dickon would look about him.
"I could take a country fellow from mine estate
But I've a fancy now for a Londoner
As brisker."
                Dickon listened with glowing eyes
While the shrewd, remembering part of his mind took in
The shabby lodging, the splendid plum-colored hose,
The hard mouth and bitter eyes of Sir Gilbert Hay.
"If he hath an estate," thought Dickon, "I'm a Dutchman
And Master Knapp is lucky to get his price,
For the purse is lean—and already he smells of wine."
But it did not matter. Nothing mattered but this,
Knave or honest, he was bound for Virginia
And needed a likely lad.
                    "Aye sir," said Dickon,
In the false, respectful voice that he knew by heart,
"If your worship will trust me, your worship shall have his
    will."
He didn't dare to wink, though he thought of it,
But his heart beat so that it almost stifled him.

When he'd left, Sir Gilbert Hay stood picking his teeth.
God's bones! 'twas a poor small victory enough
But, it might be useful, and he still knew a rogue.
"I've seen such limber fellows as that before
And, once tamed and trained, they're of service. Well, I can
    tame him."
He grinned a little, showing white even teeth.

They had been his beauty once and he still took care of
    them
Though, at thirty-eight, he'd come to dyeing his beard.
It was years since he'd played Achilles in the masque
And had the Queen's gusty notice for an instant.
"The boy's teeth gleam like a hound's. What's the springald's
    name?"
And, for twenty years, he had followed like a hound
The heels of favor and notice, often used,
Thrown a bone now and then but never quite kenneled and
    fed,
For you could not tell when he would snap at the hand.
He was false enough to be used, but he lacked cold craft.
Brave enough at a raid but bad in command,
Too lucky with women, too petulant with men,
Gulping small prizes, letting the big ones slip,
And balancing on dishonor every year.
But, to himself, he was still the sagacious man
Who wears the world like a glove on his right hand.
Knowing all dice are loaded but sure to win
With one magnificent cast of the dice at last.
And now, he had come to some credit with my lord Delaware,
An uphill business, but worth it in the end,
Worth the cold shoulder, the hourly rebuffs,
The waiting, picking one's teeth, while my lord was closeted,
"And a damned bad dinner he gave me, scanted the wine,
But, playing the tried campaigner, he warmed at last."
Only, devil take it, a knight must sail like a knight,
And the city widow could not be bled forever
Nor his own staid brother. "I must have a servingman
And, if this rogue goes off with his master's purse,

'Tis a long, salt way from London to Virginia,
And, faith, let us hope that he does—for all gold is gold."

Tick-tock,
Tick-tock,
In the Leyden Street
Down by Bell Alley
The grave faces meet,
"Welcome, neighbor Bradford!
Welcome, neighbor Keyes!
We have found a refuge,
A refuge overseas,
A good life, a hard life,
Better than we had.
We can preach and pray here.
Settle and be glad."
Tick-tock,
Tick-tock.

————

And the ships weighed anchor and put to sea,
Six from London, from Plymouth three,
A notable venture, a lusty crew
With Gates and Somers and Newport, too,
And a bold eight hundred jammed aboard
To win Virginia with spade and sword.
Their sails were white in the blue May air.
—But Dickon sailed with Delaware,
Nine months later, grumbling at fate,
For the gold would be found and he came too late.
Had he not seen bold Captain Smith,

Limping the street like a walking myth,
Still in pain from his powder-burn
But swearing, cocksbody, he would return!
For the land was a very Palestine,
Ready to flow with oil and wine
Would they send but workers over the brine,
A prize, a Canaan, a promised land!
—And Dickon felt the gold in his hand.
But his knight, by turns, blew cold and hot,
Now he would go, and now would not,
For the Wests were rogues and the voyage vain,
And then, next day, he would go again,
Shaky and dry from last night's carouse
But full of tales of his manor-house.
"And he speaks of it nobly," thought Dickon wisely,
"But he never says where it is precisely."
But, bowing and listening, day by day,
He took the measure of Gilbert Hay,
Justly reckoned for good and bad,
By the deadly eyes of a knowing lad,
The tongs for his beard and the lust for sack
And the fine, unpaid-for clothes on the back,
The dicer's courage, the drunkard's charm,
And the rags of honor that kept him warm.
For the man was false as a wormy pear
But you still could find bravadoes there.
He was wood that had rotted while it was green
But you still could see what the tree had been.
"And, if he is false," thought Dickon, "why
By the bells of St. Botolph! what am I?
For my folk will think me a scapegrace son

And, by all that they knew of it, I am one,
A runaway prentice that shames his trade
When they thought that I had my fortune made.
And I grieve for the shoulders of poor Jack Blount,
For he'll break the news and must bear the brunt.
Though I took naught—naught to call it taking,
But the two stale loaves of Tuesday's baking,
The paper of pins and the pair of hose.
—And, as God is my witness, I'd worked for those!—
There were three rose-nobles left in the till
And I looked at them, but they lie there still.
And a man may hang for a velvet cap
But I think better of Master Knapp
Though I would Jack Blount had a spryer tongue—"
He thought of the men that he'd seen hung,
Shivered an instant and faced the wind.
He might hang. But he could not have stayed behind.
And then he was sick, and then was sicker,
And his knight swore vilely and called for liquor.
"Fine, brisk weather," the sailors said,
But Dickon groaned as he held his head
—And woke, one morning, shaken and wan
To find that he had his sea-legs on
And could think of dinner and not begin
To feel the sweat creep out on his skin
At the first rank whiff of the salted meat.
He was born and bred to the London street.
He had no knowledge, except of men,
But it served him now, and it would again
As he looked about with his sparrow's eye
At rearing billow and tossing sky,

The whipping sheet and the breaker curled
And all of the whole new, strange sea-world,
Thinking, "This is a venture where some will die
But I'll take some pains that it be not I.
Nay sir, coming!"
                    He had no choice
But to run to Sir Gilbert's angry voice,
But he thought, as he helped his master dress,
"Is this a man for a wilderness?
I will serve him well and learn what I can,
But some day I shall be my own man,
Aye, and more of a man than this."
Now the doublet-points had gone amiss
And Sir Gilbert cuffed him. He took the blow
But it waked a devil he did not know
—The smiling devil of poacher Hern,
With his stolen woman, deep in the fern,
Outlaw, vagrant, rogue to the bone,
But never anyone's man but his own,
Till they hanged him duly on Gibbet Hill
While his trapped eyes glared like a fox's still
At priest and sheriff and hangman Harry
And all of the world of fetch-and-carry,
The outlier, the mutineer,
Smelling of beechmast and the deer—
"Ha," thought Sir Gilbert, hooking his sword,
" 'Tis a fledgling Cain that I've brought aboard!"
But he liked spirit, for you could break it,
And the fellow was biddable, devil take it,
And had the excellent common sense
Of never plaguing a man for pence.

"Aye, I like the fellow, in my own way,
And if he hangs, as the fellow may,
I'll be sorry for it," thought Gilbert Hay.

He swaggered on deck with his soldier's walk
And his pouncing airs of a battered hawk
And Dickon followed him, tongue in cheek,
But with something within him that was not meek,
Something that grew through the long sea-days,
A new thing, ready to seek new ways,
"Master and man
Since time began.
But some day I shall be my own man."
It jigged in his head like a ballad-rhyme
And he heard and reckoned it, biding his time.

They touched for water at the Azores
And then were off for the golden shores,
And a leaner and browner Dickon heard
The huge plans building, word by word,
The vast air-castles, stately and tall,
With the flag of England over them all
That restless gentlemen can design
With a finger dipped in the dregs of wine
When they're bored with the voyage and the endless sea
And the chicken-cooped monotony,
And one was sure he would find Cathay
And one plucked pearls from a golden strand,
And one, who was coughing his life away,
Knew he'd mend as soon as he got to land,
For the fever of landing burned like fire

In knight and hosier and bumpkin squire,
As the rumors went from lip to lip,
Buzzing their way through the crowded ship,
"Oh, a planter's life is the only life!
Though it irks a fellow to have no wife,
But, when I'm 'stablished, I'll send for Kit
And a rare good wedding we'll have of it
For she bussed me at leaving and cried salt tears.
Is it true that the heathen have devil's ears?
True? Aye, marry, notably true,
And tails that wag at their haunches, too.
But they're poor vermin and will not stand.
We'll root them up like weeds from the land,
Though their women, they say, are another thing
And woundily lecherous in the Spring.
See Tom's eyes staring! 'Twill crack my sides!
He's couched already with ten red brides!
Tom! Knowest the savage for 'Sweet, lie down'?
Nay but, neighbors—and Frankie Brown
Hath it from one of my lord's own men
Who heard while he passed him his cup again
That the way to prosper—

But, honest Wat,
Will there be gold there?

And will there not!
Didst ever hear of a heathen crew
That had no gold for their devil's due?
And it says so, too, in the clearest print,
For I had the sheet read me by Jacob Stint
And the man is a niggard but 'a reads fair
And showed me the plain black letters there,

'Gold'.
          But the fellows who came before
Will have gotten the best and richest store
And we shall go naked while they wear silk!
Nay, 'tis no use crying for that spilt milk!
Good hearts, shall we grudge a comrade's luck?
There's more than one wing to a roasted duck
And we shall have plenty or I'm a cheat,
Though Tom, there, dreams of more dainty meat.
Pish, Tom! What will your sweetheart do
When your bare half-heathens squeak 'Dad!' at you?
Nay but, neighbors, I say, I swear—
And now, good fellows, I do declare
(Peace, there! Listen! Listen to Wat!)
We be rich already and know it not!
And being—you know me—a sober man
And able to winnow wheat from bran
(Aye! We know you, Watty! Tush, listen now!)
I do judgmatically here avow
That, e'en were the gold some task to find,
It would not alter my valiant mind,
Nay, though it took me a year or twain
To reap the harvest and get the gain,
And so, 'tis my counsel we should not seek
To look for Christmas in Easter Week,
But briskly and soberly plant and hew,
Not all cock-a-hoop as the Spaniards do.
Be there pearls there? Good! Then we'll have them!
  (*Aye!*)
But perchance there are other fish to fry,
Such as woods and spices and precious gums

And other noble and dainty crumbs
As cloves and cinnamon, rare as gold,
And bringing rare prices when they are sold.
So, my word is still—let us ope our eyes
And not dash headlong at the first prize,
For there may be miracles yet unfound,
And now let us drink our fortunes round,
For we have the rabbit by the ears!"

Dickon joined in the cries and cheers,
Reading the luck of a planter's lot
In the red flushed face of honest Wat,
And seeing dimly, finished and done,
His wide plantations of cinnamon
Where the parrots—were they?—sported and flew
And the savages knelt, as savages do
(At least in broadsides sold in the street),
The wondrous future, the dream complete.
And yet, and queerly, through all the roar
He thought, "I have heard wares cried before.
'What d'ye lack? What d'ye lack?'
But the front did not always match the back."
He joined the chorus and clinked his can
But the small tick-tock in his veins began
"To be my own man. To be my own man."

And at last it was there—the longed-for land.
Broad water, with capes upon either hand,
Land—and the taste of it on the tongue.
And they all stared at it with hearts grown young,
Even the oldest, even the worn,

Like hounds that answer the huntsman's horn.
"Aye, there's your Virginia," a sailor said,
And Dickon's eyes were out of his head
And his knight looked doughty as duke or earl
With even his beard in a fresher curl.
Trees—and earth—and the soft June sky.
They came to their anchorage jauntily,
Lowered the longboat to explore
And crowded the rigging to stare ashore
And, suddenly, Dickon heard a hail
"They've come to meet us!" He ran to the rail
But the longboat, now, was a bobbing speck
And you couldn't see from the crowded deck.
He swarmed up the rigging, hand and foot,
Getting a kick from a sailor's boot,
But he hardly felt it for—yes, 'twas true.
There were four new specks on the dancing blue
Just where the line of vision fails,
Though his thumb could cover their tiny sails.
And Wat's voice crowed like a rooster, bold,
"Gold, brave hearts! They'll be crammed with gold!"

And that was the end of Dickon's youth
For, long ere sunset, they knew the truth,
Bitter as arrows, black as night.
The ships of greeting were ships in flight.
The golden men were the wreckage tossed
On the black-toothed reef where the fleet is lost,
Riddled with hunger, grey of face,
And weakly cursing the deadly place.
The fort was in ruins, the venture sped,

. . *Reprinted from the June Book-of-the-Month Club News* . . .

WESTERN STAR
By STEPHEN VINCENT BENÉT

THE extraordinary good luck of our now having the joy of this fine poem shows what it can mean to a people to have poets around. Here are both history and story telling at their simple best. Using that silver sparkle in the Western sky as his emblem, Benét has traced the onward instinct of the first American settlers. His prelude sets the tempting theme in perspective and proportion. Moving from loose, long-jointed harmonies to set stanzas of his own special skill, he plays (at first humorously, then with deeper tone) on the typical American bravura, "We don't know where we're going but we're on our way." And half heard in allure and defiance are all those whistling and chiming musics that have teased the Western race, birds, frogs, cowbells, great trains at night, and the banjo and skillet lutany of the prairie schooner.

I think that even in the prelude one can see that Stephen Benét had grown since *John Brown's Body*. But in the swift and variously modulated treatment of the tale itself one marks at once the narrator in command of his matter. The art of verse is always gorgeously superior to prose for telling a story; how instantly the reader's feeling leaps to fill in the confirming detail, and how subtly the mood required can be suggested by changes of meter. Benét tells us, in alternate episodes, the heroic enterprise of the Virginia and New England settlements. In a series of pictures with music we follow the adventures of Dickon Heron, the mercer's apprentice who runs away from London to sail for the Chesapeake, and the Lanyard family who are of the Puritan group in the *Mayflower*. It is the chronicles of America distilled in the clear crystal of the magician's vase. When the rumor runs through London taverns — "Have you heard the news of Virginia?" is the recurrent refrain — the reader himself is as one who leaps from the ale-stained bench to run outdoors and hear the drone of the ballad-singer or gape at the live Indian at the Rose and Crown—"drinks ale like a Christian." With all the cunning of his own Elizabethan gusto Stephen Benét has caught the accent and jostle of that time. Facts we had all read in

the patents and charters are, as Walt Whitman once said, "sprinkled over with light." Whether it is Raleigh in the Tower seeing his autumn sunset crossed with iron bars, or the bone-faced postmaster at Scrooby on the Great North Road — the poet brings those forlorn and stubborn visions square with our present need. He shows us that no matter how hard those oaken men tried to stay English, they became a new race unawares.

I suppose it is the briefest of modern epics, yet how much it tells and how much more it can suggest. What is thoroughly good, it is seventeenth-century courage told always (as the true poet must) from the sharpened purview of Now. When a laborer and a maidservant join in the first white wedding in America, and are one of the only two families in Virginia, the comment is, "Where do you start when you start counting F.F.V.'s?" When the stern and hidebound Pilgrim zealots are almost within glimpse of "Somebody" in the woods of Massachusetts Bay, but find only warm embers or shadows behind the tree, our sympathy is as much with the savage as with the Saltonstall. May it be so in our behalf when the epic of our own day comes to ink. And through the whole great ballad, for it is in gist a ballad of a dozen woven tunes, like the whistling imp-song of spring woods on the James, is the word and memory of those who perished, the riddle-word *Croatan.* Here are recaptured, in his fine phrase, "lost Iliads of the forest."

It is quite possible that Stephen Benét had revisions and enlargements in mind; in the luxury of the artist still holding his picture in fancy he might honestly have said, "It isn't finished." But I think it more happily complete than even he could have guessed and after all America itself isn't finished. The theme and the music are both of power that suggests Whitman again: "the sky o'erarches here." The meaning and purpose are well accomplished in the reader's mind. He comes with a thrill toward the end on a talisman:—

"Remember the names of
    the outcast and the
    stranger.
'I will have none of this
    exile and this stranger
For his face is not like
    my face and his speech
    is strange'
You have denied Amer-
    ica with that word."

He has raked the camp-fire embers of American story, and found them still live coal.

CHRISTOPHER MORLEY

In accordance with a suggestion made by a number of our subscribers, this monthly reprint from the Book-of-the-Month Club *News* is printed in this format so that it can be pasted, if desired, to the flyleaf of the book.

They had eaten adders and their own dead
And the lank survivors were bones of men.

And yet, they went back, to build again.

Yet write one fresh name in honor there,
Thomas West, my lord Delaware.
He was neither to love the land nor stay,
But he showed cold courage in a dark day,
Quick decision and instant act
And a will that matched with the iron fact
Though he was not to end as he began
But a sick and self-excusing man,
Fleeing the land on his doctor's orders
And leaving others to be its warders.
For, though his titles were broad and fair
And he was Governor Delaware,
The flux and the scruvy were not impressed.
—Well, he knew his own constitution best.
Governed after by deputy
And, on his way back again, died at sea.
A mixture of merits, as most men are,
But touched, that once, by a cold, sure star.
He was tested then and he met the test.
—We acknowledge the quality, Thomas West.

Now, he came to Jamestown, a burly savior,
With a rod in pickle for misbehavior,
And they listened docilely, old and new,
To the words he spoke and the plans he drew,
Sensibly, soldierly, the new broom
That means to sweep the dust from the room.

—It was aching June, the honeysweet,
And an idle drum in the forest beat,
Casual, distant, a low, dim sound
But telling its news for miles around,
"White men—back again—white men—more.
Is it peace or war? Is it peace or war?"
It throbbed like a pulse in Dickon's blood
As he stood and sweated, sweated and stood,
Till my lord had finished his brief oration
And the chaplain prayed for King and nation.
"England—but this is no English wood
And the river's name is Solitude
Not the James, for it winds and smiles
Through vine-hung, tree-embowered miles
That never knew ax or English rose
Where the naked men go bending their bows—
A huge, smooth serpent, ancient and slow,
And waiting, waiting for us to go.
For man is little, under this sky,
Man is little and soon gone by.
Who cares now if we live or die?
The very earth grins mockingly.
We can lift our voices and cheer King James,
But these dead in the ground—had they English names?"

The thing was over, the men dispersed;
The new men, anxious to know the worst,
Shyly trying to draw aside
The men who had lived, who had not died,
And asking the questions that new men ask,
With the dry lips set in a jaunty mask,

Friendly, garrulous and forlorn,
While the old hands chewed on their own bleak scorn.
They might be damned and they thought they were
But 'twas something to harrow a newcomer
With fables that made his blood run cold
While the true, long horror remained untold
And would not be told till Judgment Day.

Dickon looked for Sir Gilbert Hay
And heard him answer young Terret's quip
With a pleasant laugh and a steady lip,
"Nay, we went barer in Ireland, Jack,
And what you need is a cup of sack.
Tush, man, never be down at cheek
Or I'll throw no dice with you for a week.
There's a sound fort here—or there has been one."
And pink-cheeked Terret, the younger son,
With his bright colt's face and his youngster's walk,
Drew visible strength from the battered hawk.
Things couldn't be bad when such men laughed.
"Aye, sir. Well, we'll meet for an evening draught."
Sir Gilbert smiled him out of sight,
Beard cocked boldly and dog-teeth white,
And then the change came over his face
That comes to a man who has run a race
Shrewdly and cunningly and unfairly
And yet is beaten, although but barely,
As he stared with his close-lipped gamester's stare
At running river and blowing air
And the sprouted ruins of James his town,
The broken cabins, the gate cast down.

"I have cheated the devil once or twice
But it seems that he plays with loaded dice.
Gold?" he muttered, and caught his breath.
"The damned place stinks of fever and death."

———————

We are humble men.
We English, living in peace in red-tiled Leyden,
In the quiet city that Alva could not take,
Printers, stocking-weavers and fustian-makers,
We are humble men.

We are quiet men.
Our presence does not jangle the life of the city.
They stared a little, at first, but they have ceased staring.
We are used to its ways now, we try to be good neighbors.
We are quiet men.

All that we ask is quiet and God's guidance.
For that we left our England, wrenching our roots up,
The thick taproots, the slow roots of hind and yeoman,
For that we left brisk, quarreling Amsterdam,
Seeking our own way.

And the days come and go and the bells of Bell Alley
Ring, the exile's bells of the foreign city.
But our day is God's, not one city's or another's,
Our strength is in God and God is our great warden,
He will not fail us.

And yet, with each day, we know ourselves exiled
And our children are young but grow. Will they grow God's
    children?

Already the foreign tongue is so easy for them,
And we live in the country but we are not of the country,
We are strangers, still.

It is easy to melt and mix, to sink down, grow sleepy,
To be recalled "Yes, my grandmother was English.
They came for their faith, I think—I have heard her stories.
But she was old and I do not quite remember."
It is easy to fall from God.

Each day we heave a stone, each day more difficult,
Each day we live in peace but a peace that trembles,
Each Sabbath we meet in Zion, and yet our Zion
Is a green field granted by others, may be removéd
And is not steady.

We are quiet men.
But God has tried us and stricken us and recovered us.
He has shown us grace and terror and things inescapable
And the long years are forging us iron heartstrings.
We shall answer His will like iron when He proclaims it.
We are waiting men.

————————

"Have you finished your stint, Humility?"

"Yes, mother."

The dark-haired woman looked at the neat, small stitches,
While the child watched anxiously.

"Is it well done, mother?"
"Well enough, child, but you must not be proud of it.
It is wrong to be proud of the trifling work of our hands.

Our task is to make them acceptable to God.
Are you sure you know that, Humility?"

                              "Yes, mother,
And I am not proud of it. May I show it to Father?"

"Yes, child, if there is no sinful pride in your heart."

The child nodded gravely and went back to her work
And Katharine Lanyard wished that she loved her better.
She was Matthew's child and should be easy to love,
Matthew's and her own sister's. "I will pray
Again and the door at last shall be opened to me."
But it was not opened. The child was meek and quiet,
Gentle, too, and made no noise in the house,
But, every now and then, she would look like Rose,
The Rose who had taken Matthew and lay dead
And, in spite of death, still was first and always first
As you could see when Matthew looked at the child.
"But my womb has been opened now and I shall bear.
I shall bear him sons, a strong harvest, for I am strong.
For a while I thought I might not, and that was dread,
Though I could have borne it and accepted it
As being God's will—aye, even the loathly stares
Of the woman Billington and her chuckling eyes.
And I heard her call me a vinegar-virgin once
But I walked past and she did not know that I heard."

She moved about the room, quick-handed and deft,
It was better kept, and she knew it, than Rose had kept it.
For what Katharine Lanyard did, she did with a strong
Concentrate passion, almost a martyrdom.

She had learned early she wasn't the pretty one
And shut her lips on the knowledge and gone her way.
She hated the greasy pot and cleaned it well
Where Rose, for all her fragileness, didn't mind,
There being pots in the world as well as lovers.
But Katharine was different metal.
She could be burned or burn but she must have
Something that used her, wore her and absorbed her,
Something that was not easy, so must be right,
And she struggled in the strict bond of her faith
And the bond of being a woman, in a time
When women's bonds were more closely knit upon them,
Dark-haired, dark-eyed, with passion in the eyes,
Burningly chaste, sure all her ways were right,
And yet, in spite of self-torment, not unhappy.
Such people are not. They may make you unhappy
If you cross their creed, but that is another thing.
They will always have contempt for the ripe, smooth fruit
And get their satisfactions out of the stone,
As Katharine did.
                    She had married the man she wanted,
Though she would not have put it so, not on the rack,
And now she carried the first of his sons for God.
She did not sing, as she moved about the room,
But her sure hands did their work with a swift thoroughness.

The child on the stool,
Mouse-brown, mouse-quiet, with quick, fragile color,
The eyes of children who are old for their years
And a secret spring of gaiety in her heart,
Thought her long child's thoughts.

It was nice to be clean and fed.
Have her hair combed and her face washed every day
And not have Father worried when he came home.
She'd been very stupid about the stint at first,
But she was learning—and she'd almost forgotten
The funny words that the Billington children said
Because she didn't play with them any more.
Sometime they would all be burnt up in a big fire
Because God wished it, but they didn't know about it
And she wouldn't be allowed to see it, probably.
She wasn't allowed to see things like that now
Nor hear about elves and hangings from Mother Billington,
But she was clean and fed and Aunt Kate was here.
She'd had a lovely mother before Aunt Kate
But that one died and was put in a box in the ground
And afterwards went to the New Jerusalem.
And Aunt Kate was water and soap and tidy things,
Scary, sometimes, when she prayed, but you needn't listen.
You could make your face look as if you were listening
And think about honey-on-bread and little bugs
And the chattering, tame squirrel the cobbler had,
And then, somehow, by looking as if you were listening,
Get into a small, good place you kept to yourself
That even Father never had known about.
You couldn't explain it, for it wasn't in words,
But things were nice there, and it was all green and brown
And little and warm, as a mouse's cubbyhole.
There were lots of little dishes and little scissors
And you could play with all of them, all the time,
And God saw the small, good place but He wasn't angry,
Though elsewhere He looked with a great and burning eye

And you had to be very careful.

         He was big
As thunder and terrible as a horse's hoofs.
He looked at the wicked and gathered them up in heaps
And threw them into the everlasting fire
And they burned and crackled and made a bad smell like
  feathers.
It wasn't any use trying to hide from Him.
He was always looking at everyone in the world,
So you had to know His election or else you'd burn.
—And sometimes dream about burning—and wake up
With the bedclothes slipped and your throat too scared to cry,
Feeling the heat and hearing the angry hoofs
And thinking, dolefully, of the smell like feathers.
But you mustn't waken the grown ones in the big bed.
You must lie on your back and shiver and feel the flame,
And then, after a while, the small, good place would come,
And things would be green and brown and you could sleep.

          So, like the vine,
That grows through the split of the rock, and yet will grow,
And gets its food and its light because it must,
The child built her own child's world with the tools she had
On the premises given, and it was a real world,
Though Katharine Lanyard would not have found it so.
And Matthew came and they welcomed him.

            And, after,
When he sat for a moment with the child on his knees,
Katharine thought, "Nay, I do not begrudge. I do not.
How can I, when I also bear him a child?
I wish to tell him. I wish to tell him now."
But it was not just and she knew it and denied it.

"The child would show you her stint," she said, with strict
  justice.

———

Dickon Heron looked around
His three rough acres of granted ground
And rested a moment on his hoe
At the end of a tobacco-row.
—A queer, wild plant with a bitter leaf
And the lusty appetite of a thief,
But Master Rolfe thought it worth the trying,
And he'd try anything new but dying.

He was three years older as years are told,
But old for Virginia, ages old,
For he'd seen them come and he'd seen them die,
The raw men out of each new supply,
And now he was one of the seasoned few
That Death had given a stroke or two,
Tried with the cold fit and the hot,
With bleak starvation and arrow-shot,
And then let go, with an air that said,
"Remember me, while you eat your bread."

"Aye, I remember you," Dickon thought,
"And shall while my bones remember aught,
Remember my first cold wintertide
When a hundred and fifty of us died
And our Governor found that an eastbound ship
Was the one sure cure for Jamestown pip.
And, faith, by the time that he got aboard,
There was little left of the noble lord!

And I'll remember Sir Gilbert Hay,
With his sunken eyes and his beard gone grey,
Calling for dice with his last breath,
The dog-wolf, snarling back at Death,
And swearing he'd leave me a thousand pound
If I saw him buried in clean, dry ground.
And he lied. And he knew that I knew he lied.
But I watched beside him until he died,
For do I not owe him my fortune here?"
He smiled at that and the smile was queer,
Neither embittered nor desperate
But the flirt of a sparrow's head at Fate,
"I have cooled my heels in Jamestown jail
And tasted the justice of Thomas Dale
And there is a mastiff—old Ironlungs,
With his pretty devices of bodkined tongues,
Whippings and hangings and laws so dread
They could hang a man for pissing his bed.
But men will labor when they're in fear
And he's no bad dog for the kennel here.
He may carry a rope in either hand
But the old Dutch mastiff gave us land.

Oh, Master Knapp, do you wake or sleep?
Can you see from Chepe, can you see from Chepe?
For I think, if you could, you'd be well-content
With your runaway prentice's punishment,
Aye, and deem him already in hell.
And yet I live. And I like it well."

And he stopped, surprised, for that was true,
Though he could not tell how it was he knew,

But it stared in his face like woman or ghost,
The sudden knowledge that did not boast,
Prophesy, palter or explain
But spoke its message to flesh and brain,
"Man is little under this sky,
Man is little and soon gone by,
But, while there is breath in me, here stand I.
This is my land, my gallows-rope,
My exultation and my hope.
I have pledged no oath, I have made no vow,
But this is the land for me, I trow."
He wiped his brow with a sunburnt hand,
"Aye," he muttered, "they're fine and grand,
Knight and lawyer and all their band
But I think it is we who plant the land.
And now I must look for Jemmy Crews
For the new ship's in and there will be news,
Pray God they've shipped us a plow or so,
'Twould save much labor of spade and hoe,
But they're liker to send us silkworms—aye—
And why they send what they send—God knows why!
'Tis a deep and marvelous mystery.
For the last new man they quartered on me
Was a Hamburg hatter who cursed in German
And was most uncommonly blest with vermin.
Well, the poor rogue's dead of the bleedy measles.
But why was he sent? To make hats for weasels?"

He swore like a trooper and dropped his hoe.
It was always so. It was always so.
For, mounting the hillock, up the track,

Was a man with a bundle on his back.
"They've landed their men while I dream and drowse
And now I will have to share my house,
My fine, plank cabin, near six-feet wide,
With some rat from the London waterside
Or else a mammy-sick newcome loon
Who doesn't know wampum from puccoon.
But, body of God, there's a woman, too!"
He stared, agape, for it couldn't be true.
There were women in Jamestown but they were rare,
Yet the thing had skirts and was walking there,
Skirts and a step that did not tire
While Jemmy Crews played the gallant squire,
But she was not looking at Jemmy Crews
As "Dickon!" he bawled. "Here be friends and news!"
And Dickon ran, though his legs felt weak,
To kiss Jack Blount upon either cheek,
Hold him and grip him and think, "Alack!
Poor lad, poor devil, poor fat poor Jack!
Could you not have stayed? Must you come to die?"
And then turn with a flourish, laughingly,
Smelling of earth and the sunburnt South,
To kiss Jack's sister's merry young mouth
And note that she stood as tall as he
Ere the fever of talking took the three.

It was two months later that they were wed.
She could do no other, when Jack lay dead.
And he had sickened the second week
While Dickon watched him with eyes grown bleak.
"Aye, I know the signs, though no doctor I,

And the stout, flushed fellows always die.
And I would to God that it might not be,
For the poor fool came for love of me
And all I can do for him, once he's sped,
Is to see the girl keeps her maidenhead."
But that was more easy to say than do,
For the hounds will answer the view-halloo,
And some of them were not cleanly hounds
That even Dale's laws could not keep in bounds.
He had chased one fellow with oath and knife
While poor Jack Blount still clung to his life,
Threatened a second and drubbed another,
"And Jemmy Crews plays the elder brother,
Grinning upon her with lanthorn jaws
And bringing her mulberries in his paws.
For her mouth is merry—her heart is good—
And, to her, 'tis the ballad of Babes in the Wood,
Which I would to God I had never heard."
He gazed at the girl like an anxious bird,
At the smooth, bright hair and the merry smile
And the candid eyes that had no guile.
"She can wed—aye, must—and that would be best,
But not with a fellow like Nicky Test.
He can deck himself like Jack-of-the-Green
But the man was a thief and the maid is clean.
And Jemmy, God knows, is an honest lump
—And comes about her, wagging his rump,
Till I marvel she does not kick the fellow—
And Dickon, my lad, are you green and yellow?
Does it matter to you who calls the turn?
And how is it any of your concern?"

And yet it was, though he'd not admit
The stinging smart of the arrow-hit
As by field and cabin and sick man's bed
The swift and casual courtship sped
With a few small jests and a word or two
And each one knowing the other true,
Through the burning Summer and the shared toil,
The truth, the harvest of the soil.

She was no heroine, Alice Blount,
But a girl who would take her wounds in front,
Laugh while she could, cry when she must,
And share while she lived, be it crumb or crust.
The house would be clean, while it was her house,
But she'd leave a crumb for the kitchen-mouse
For he made her laugh, with the bold and sly
Stare of his black, unwinking eye
And the way his whiskers stood on end.
She was honest lover and merry friend,
Sound as a pippin at the heart
And, like the pippin, both sweet and tart,
For the sun might parch and the wind might blow,
But, where she was planted, she would grow,
Trim as cherry, stubborn as pine,
And sturdy as the blackberry-vine
When the weather kills both lily and box.
Her flowers were pinks and four-o'clocks.

They were well-mated, Dickon and she,
Though not, perhaps, as they'd thought they'd be
When they thought of mating in London town

Where love went gallantly up and down.
Love with the posy and the rose,
A ballad-singer in scarlet hose.
But here was wild earth and burning sun,
The toil that was done and never done,
The sick man, picking the coverlet,
And the brief cool breath when the sun had set,
Before the enormous night began
To show how small were woman and man
By the shine of its aching, countless stars.
Then they talked and laughed but the words were sparse
And lost themselves like birds in the night.
And yet, there were moments of swift delight
Like the purple grapes on the muscadine,
Swelling, ready to burst in wine,
The rich, dark summer of the vine.
The odd, clear moments that change the sky
When they looked at each other merrily
And thought, for an instant that had no span,
"I can trust this woman. I trust this man.
I have given no pledge. I have made no vow
But life will bring it about somehow
And it will taste of grapes and the sun
And be better than sleep when the day is done."
—Two stray sparrows of London eaves,
Lost in a forest of painted leaves.

They went to the church when they'd buried Jack,
And, that same evening, he brought her back,
With a ring on her finger of silvered dross
And parson's blessing on gain and loss.

—For life is simple, stripped to the bone,
And the hearth must be swept and the seed be sown
Though grief has been and though grief will be.
Then in came the neighbors, by two and three,
Corporal Tolley and Andy Moon,
Bringing the skin of a fine raccoon,
Tail and all for a wedding-gift,
And Goodwife Moon had sent her a shift,
But could not come, though she sent goodwill,
For this was the day of her ague-chill.
But the shift was linen and scarcely worn.
Yet most of the guests brought fruit and corn.
Little enough, for their store was small,
But freely given by one and all,
For a lawful wedding must have good cheer
Though this might be another starving-year.
And when they beheld lean Jemmy Crews
With his red-faced gift of a fat wild goose,
They roared at Jemmy and asked him, sweetly,
If it was his own brother he'd shot so featly.
"Nay, good neighbor—the moonstruck elf
Hath plucked up the valor to pluck himself,
And who shall deem it a deed unworthy?"
—The jests of the simple, sweaty and earthy.
When the tears of mirth run down the cheek
Of the folk who may be dead in a week
And never know when the hour will strike
That ends both labor and jests alike.
They were gone at last, with a parting cup,
Though one voice still trolled, "Wantons, come up!"
Where Corporal Tolley, with wambling strides,

Confided his liking for new-made brides
And his hope that he, too, might marry soon
To the night, the stars and the man-in-the-moon,
Till at last, like a cricket, he chirped no more,
And Dickon bolted the cabin door
With one last glance of his sparrow's eye
At the full moon, flooding the midnight sky.
"And Jack lies cold in his grave, poor Jack,
And yet, no wishing will bring him back,
For I did what I could and I have my life,
That, and Alice, my new-wed wife,
Though she well may think me a rogue, poor lass,
When she thinks of all that has come to pass,
Aye, and that which is still to do
That walks like a fire between us two
—A canting rascal all chockablock
With getting the girl stripped down to her smock—
And make her woman I must and can
For I take no shame in being a man
And yet, by heaven and my heart's root,
I love the creature from head to foot
And would chop my hand would it spare her sorrow—
But still—will she think me a knave, tomorrow?"
He smiled at her as he raked the fire
And the smile was youth and youth's desire
And yet was mixed with a certain ruth
That is not always found in youth,
And she thought, as her hair streamed down on her shift,
"My body is all my wedding gift,
And this is my wedding, and it is strange.
But, once I have given, I do not change.

And yet—does he love me? 'Twas all so swift—
Dickon! You had not to marry me!"
"Why, no, my Alice—dear Alice—" said he,
Taken aback for once, and then
With the gipsy mirth in his eyes again,
"But marriage, they say, is a noble state.
And dost not see our service of plate
And the Turkey carpet spread on the floor?
And what could a husband give you more?
And—ah, love me a little, dear Alice, sweet Alice,
For, an you do not, all the world is false.
And 'tis hard for a maid so young, God wot!
But how may I live, if you love me not?"
Then she put her hand on his naked breast
And they knew they were one, for worst and best,
And the hearth-fire glimmered on fruit and corn
Till the long night failed and the day was born.

———

And we look back, and see how the thing was done
And, looking back, think, "So, of course, it must be."
And are wrong by a million miles, and never see
The daily living and dying, under the sun.

For they did not know what would happen. No one knew.
No one knew, though the men in England planned,
Planned with cunning of brain and strength of hand,
And their plans were deer-tracks, fading out in the dew.

They planned for gold and iron, for silk and wood,
For towns and settled farming and steady things,

And an Indian pipe puffed out its blue smoke-rings,
And, where they had made their plans, the tobacco stood.

And those who came were resolved to be Englishmen,
Gone to world's end, but English every one,
And they ate the white corn-kernels, parched in the sun,
And they knew it not, but they'd not be English again.

They would try, they would swear they were, they would
    drink the toast,
They would loyally petition and humbly pray
And over them was another sort of day
And in their veins was another, a different ghost.

For the country is where the life is, not elsewhere.
The country is where the heart and the blood are given.
They could swear to be English by every oath under heaven.
It did not alter the country by a hair.

———————

And now, the ships
Go back and forth, with Middlesex, Surrey, Devon,
A dozen English counties crowding aboard
For the long voyage—and the constant, relentless death,
Ever at heel—You can count the roll as you like
But your chance of living was something like one in eight
Through those first fifteen-odd years of the colony
And something like seven thousand lives were paid,
Paid, and a line drawn under, and canceled out,
That eleven hundred should live when those years were done.
On the other hand, if you lived through your first year,

You were likely to go on living and get your land.
(Land! And my own! And black earth, fertile as God!)
And they came,
London, Liverpool, Bideford, Bristol, Hull,
The "Duty" boys, the poor children of the parishes,
The hundred maids sent over by Edwin Sandys,
Priced each at a hundred and fifty pounds of tobacco
And guaranteed pure maidens.
The idle boys and men who followed the Court
To Newmarket races, getting in the way,
And the King complained about them, and they were sent,
The convicts, marched to the ships through a jeering crowd,
While the fifes played, "Through the wood, laddie",
The folk who bound themselves for a term of years
For the price of the passage, the indentured servants,
Who were given a hat and a twenty-shilling gun,
And, if they lived, might rise to be burgesses,
The free men, paying their passage and starting clear,
The few younger sons of gentry with good names,
And they were as bold as any but they were few,
For no one strain came to settle this first Virginia,
But rather—you hewed a lump of English earth,
With grass and oak-stump, beetle and grub and bee,
With one white admiral to a dozen ants,
And they all came, and, as chance took them, they lived or
    died,
But the contented and portly stayed behind
Or came for a while and went back and their names are lost.
For the wild land was not broken by frozen men
Or by those who would always live in their father's pockets,
Such men come later on, when the thing is done,

And show how all things must be as they always were,
And they must have common sense, they say so themselves,
But, oddly enough, they never settle a wilderness
And never will.
                    And meanwhile, back in England,
The Company went on, as companies do,
With split and cabal and faction and new broom
And all the various troubles of all companies,
When we've spent so much—and yet we're still in the red—
And we'll get So-and-so in and try this and that
And next year will show a profit—but it doesn't.
The bickering meetings, the questions asked by investors,
The new, bland, wily prospectus for the new loan.
And Sir Thomas Smyth, old, burdened, angry and hurt,
Is down at last and Warwick and Sandys are up,
And we need not follow the cockpit quarrels they had,
For Sandys and Warwick are to split in their turn,
The staggering Company finally gasp its last,
And the Crown take over bankruptcy and colony,
Hardly in tyranny but because it must,
For who else could assume the burden?
                                    Nevertheless
We must praise both Sir Thomas Smyth and Sir Edwin
    Sandys
In spite of all the hard words they gave each other.
They tried the impossible and failed at last
And did not fail, for the work was not done in vain,
Though it did not grow as they planned.
                            And now, in Jamestown,
The Company still rules and the raw men die,
But there's peace for a while, a blue tobacco-peace

With the Indians and their sleepy and ancient chief,
For John Rolfe has been married to Pocahontas,
Feeling his heart unto her most strangely moved
—The second of the three wives that he is to wed
Ere the Indians take his scalp in '23—
And few men ever crowded more life in a life
Than this sober-tongued experimenter who took
Shipwreck, hunger and marriages in his stride
And made tobacco king of Virginia
For a century and more.
You may think of him as Pocahontas's husband.
He was rather more than that and his seed still lives,
And we would do well to fence the small plot of garden,
Where, in hose and doublet, he planted the Indian weed.

Now listen to another, graver tune,
Wrung from the oaken hearts of humble men.

———————

O God, the refuge of our fears,
Our buckler and our stay,
Within whose sight the rolling years
Are but a single day,
Behold us now, like Israel's band,
Cast forth upon the wave,
And may Thy strong and aweful hand
Be still outstretched to save!

It was over now, the living in the Dutch town,
The hard fare, the great labor, the quiet years,
The uneasy security, the exiled days,

The slow, difficult change from the life of husbandmen
To the trade-life, the town-life, the life of money and cloth.
They had seen themselves grow older and some grow broken,
And still with no sure future.
They had seen their children stunted by poverty
Beginning to change, to forget, as children will,
"Dirk Jans thinks it little sin to play at ball
And Annetje Pieters wears ruffles of Mechlin lace.
Aye, father, I know. Aye, mother, I am obedient.
But I thought no harm of talking to Captain Kieft
And the boys all say 'Donder und blitzen!' 'Tis just a saying.
And, mother, if Hendrik asks me, what may I say?"
—There never were children who did not say some such
    words—
But these were folk who believed in one thing so passionately
They would die ere they saw it broken.

                                    And they saw,
The leaders, no swift, spectacular martyrdom
(That they could have borne) but a long, grey wearing out
Under the endless trickle of alien years
These things—and the ending of the Dutch truce with
    Spain . . .
Thousands more coming, the slaughter in the night,
And what they saw, they saw
With the humble, stupendous arrogance of men
Who are quite sure God is with them.
Now, for God and land, they were going across the seas.

Methinks I hear a direful sound,
Proclaiming from the sky
That those whom Adam's chains have bound

Eternally must die.
Yet, to my soul, the voice is sweet
And gracious as the dew.
For God must winnow men like wheat
That He may save a few.

And yet—they had lived in Leyden eleven years,
There was street and house and habit that they must leave,
All the bonds of familiar custom—and more than these,
The friends, the flesh of their flesh,
Knitted to them by bone and sinew, knitted to them
By the burning peace of shared Sabbaths and quiet prayers.
For it was the boldest and strongest who were to go,
Not all, and Pastor Robinson was to stay,
The man who had been their pillar of fire and cloud,
Gentle, tolerant, steadfast, the dear saint
Who spread his wings above them and gave them rest.
There were good men who went but none who were quite
    John Robinson
And they were to miss him sorely.
                            Now, at Delft Haven,
The two bands parted with fervency and tears.
They might meet again, they might never meet again,
And the large-eyed, solemn children prayed with their elders,
On the *Speedwell's* rocking deck
And Pastor Robinson blessed them from the shore.
Then the ropes were cast off, and suddenly
There was clear water between the ship and the land,
For the tide would not wait and that was the last leave-taking
For many, on bark or land.
And William Bradford remembers and sets it down,

Years later, the tears and the passionate embraces,
The night of little sleep before the sailing,
The kneeling crowd on the shore,
And the last, hard wrench when they knew the thing begun.
A man, writing down, years later, but remembering
With the very blood of his heart.
"But they knew they were pilgrims and looked not much on
    these things,
They lifted their eyes to the heavens, their dearest country,
And quieted their spirits."
                              And it was so.

With Gideon's sword and David's harp,
We march across the main
And though the blast blow keen and sharp,
Our God shall yet sustain,
To work His burning judgments still,
His mercies to adore
And build the Zion of His will
Where none hath stood before.

———————

"Are we going, father?"
                              "Yes, Humility."
He looked at her for a moment with a stiff mouth
"I had thought," he said, weighing the words, "that you
    might stay
With your mother's people—but—and we could send later—
But—"
        She smiled at him. "But you could not have thought
    so, father.

Not truly."

       "No," he said, gravely. "Not truly. No."

"I can do such a lot of things," she said, childishly,
"And I'm fourteen and the oldest."

           "It is not that."

"Oh, father, I know but—Is it a noble ship?
And where will we sleep and how will we say our prayers?
And can Devoted take her little porringer?
She'll cry if she doesn't—oh dear—and there's Martin cry-
   ing—
I must go to him—"

          She flitted out of the room
With two bright pink spots in her cheeks and her eyes shining
While Matthew Lanyard looked after her, anxiously.
There were four other children now in the house
And he was just with them all, or tried to be,
But this one still was the maid that Rose had loved.

He was thirty-three and a master carpenter
And the work and the days and the house went well enough
But he had made up his mind and would not change,
For this was not Zion.

          It was hard to trace
The slow sure growth of convictions from the seed
Till they harden and are like armor—and yet, it happens.
And when it happens to men of Matthew's kind,
You have a force in the world.

          It was real to him, now,
Real as adz and hammer and clenching nail,

The true Zion, the Zion that must be.
He had tested each joist and beam and found them sound
And that by his own heart's testing, not Katharine's
  word.
It was all foursquare and the work of a master workman,
And neither priest nor noble had built it high
But God who respected no persons, strong, strange God,
Who hurt a man to his dying but saved his soul.
Now, it must be brought to be.
                              "Yes, and it is we
Who shall build it, not the gaudy and the fine,
For God has already judged them and cast them out,
He has judged them from the beginnings of the world."
And that, too, was definite and a man could trust it.
He had wondered, in the beginning. He did not know,
For God had spoken to him,
In the death of Rose, in Katharine, in ten thousand
Small, daily meaningful judgments, and still spoke.
God had raised him up and made him a master workman.
And now God's house and kingdom must be built.
—He saw the walls arisen, the walls of God,
And his big hands clenched to do the work they were made
  for.

Katharine Lanyard came in with the boy, Elias,
The boy with his father's looks but thinner, slighter,
And with the dark, devoted eyes she loved.
She looked her question.
                        "Aye. We will go," he said,
"Though not all in the first essay." Her fingers tightened
And she felt the boy's thin shoulder flinch for an instant.

After supper they sat quietly for a space,
Being one in this, as they were not always one.
He said, "I have seen the terms and a hardish bargain,
For we labor seven years for the common stock,
But then 'tis to be divided. Well, it's their money,
The merchants', and we must bear with them, willy-nill.
I have talked to Master Cushman. The man's perplexed
With press of business but seemeth a godly man."

She said, "Will they all be our folk?"

                              He smiled gravely,
"Nay, Kate—yet some. I have sounded Isaac Allerton,
He will go—aye, and William Mullins and Diggory Priest."

"I like not Diggory Priest!"

                              "You are wrong, wife Kate.
'Tis an honest soul, though confused on some points of doc-
     trine.
And the folk from Leyden are full of abounding grace,
Yea, folk to cleave to, I think. Yet there must be others.
I have heard of a Captain Standish who is to come,
A good, tried soldier, they say."

                              "But hath he the Word?"

"Now, wife, if the man be a soldier, e'en let him be one.
'Twill be well to have at least one man skilled in arms
For most of us are not so."

                              "We have arms from God!"

"Aye, Kate, but the savages have bows that shoot."

He sighed a little, knowing that she was trusty,
But knowing also the smoky, relentless will

That drew its line so swiftly 'twixt black and white
And had no compromise in it anywhere,
Not even with Elias, her first-born son.
Though she understood Elias better than he,
For the boy was strange, at times, with his darkling eyes
His nose in a book and his quick docile answers.
"And would I the boy were a brawling fellow? Nay,
And yet I hardly know him."

                     Then the thought passed.
They were going.

              "Let us pray for guidance," he said.
They knelt on the floor and prayed.
And Matthew Lanyard saw Zion, built foursquare.
But Katharine a refuge of saints, and the saints her seed.

In the other room,
The moon shone and Humility lay awake
Though the children who shared it with her were long in
    dreams.
She wondered how it would be to sleep on a ship.
But she wasn't afraid, though Elias was afraid.
She was sorry for Elias but knew he was
And Father shouldn't know it if she could help it.
And, down the street,
"Aye, souls," cackled Mother Billington to her gossips,
"When you see me next 'twill be with plumes on my head
And Son Jacky rich as a prince."

                    She cried in her mug
For the husband dead three years—oh, the poor, staunch man,
And who would have thought that a rheum could take him off
And coughed so hard, at the end, it was pain to hear him,

For he would not even relish the good clean ale,
But that was done—though she wept whenever she thought
    of it,
And now there was Young Jacky and the grandchildren,
The young, bold rogues—and, if he could find no work,
'Twas better sailing the seas than cutting purses,
Aye, even with long-nosed Puritans aboard.
She liked not the smell of them but there would be others,
Good, honest, hearty souls to leaven the lump,
"And, if it be whine and pray, I'll whine with the best.
For a voyage is soon enough spent, but land is land,
And Jacky—bless him!—'twill do him no hurt, for once,
To sweat without strong waters to make him sweat,
For the boy is as good as bread—and once he's quit
Of the idle fellows who dice at the 'Goat and Keys'—
And, poor boy, who would blame him—and yet, 'tis pity,
For all that he drinks with have not his good heart
And they do misguide him—and so it is better so—
For the chick has a great, proud spirit and clever wits
And will surely be notable in a new land."

She sighed. The Aldgate Ward would be hard to leave
Though she'd dearly love to gaze at an Indian,
"Aye, and scrape you to death with clam-shells, they do say.
But, an they try it with me, they'll find me an armful.
Only who'll go to my man's grave on a fine, warm Sunday?
And I'll miss my gossips—and there'll be no humming ale—
Nay, the clear, cold sea-water, swashing up and down—"
But she'd talked it over with Ellen, Jacky's wife,
And, if they went, how could she stay behind?

And yet, it was not till the sixteenth of September
That the *Mayflower* sailed at last, after two false starts.
Twice they'd set out, and twice the *Speedwell* leaked.
She was overmasted. They had to give her up
And with her some score or so of would-be Pilgrims
Who, thinking it over, decided that after all
And perhaps next time and God be with you, my friends,
But we think we'll go back to London—and, when they got
    there,
Felt, doubtless, that queer blend of relief and shame
Which comes to those who make sensible decisions.
"I'd risk myself—but there's my wife and the boy.
I'm a valuable man. I can do as much here."
—And after a while, we are sure that we have been sensible
And the sting of it dies away.
                      And yet one wonders,
What they thought, later.
                          We know what one man thought,
For he wrote it down and we can read it today,
Robert Cushman, the nervous, bewildered shade
Who had been their agent in London, talked with the mer-
    chants,
Striven with the ten thousand petty cares
That vex such agents, trying to satisfy
Merchants and voyagers and pleasing neither.
He was doing his best, he was always doing his best,
And Mr. Weston was really a splendid man,
And everything would go right, if they'd just agree.
No, the terms weren't hard. They just didn't understand.
But—so many things to look to— We can hear
The plaintive, bewildered voice, the scratching pen,

"The beer—we should have bought the beer in Kent
But now we cannot without prejudice
And we're still short three hundred pounds or so
And Mr. Weston's in an angry fume
Since we do not agree with his conditions.
Why can we not? You deem me negligent.
Why did you trust me, then? but let it pass.
And now comes Mr. Martin, simple man,
Treats me not good enough to wipe his shoes
And calls the merchants bloodsuckers.

My head!

And we must sell some butter at a loss,
And then the beer. We've paid too much for it,
And the whole work goes tottering and awry,
For violence will break all—"

And they wrote him back.

And Mr. Weston, that businesslike promoter,
Was angry indeed and washed his hands of them.
But, at least, the voyage began, and then, alack,
They were barely out of harbor when it happened
And the water began to rush through the *Speedwell's* planks,
As it were into a mole hole, and Robert saw it.
And when he saw it, knew that he'd had enough.
"For half our victuals will be eaten up,
I think, ere we leave England. My poor head!
I do the actions of a living man
Yet I am but as dead—and then the beer
We might have had—and yet God's will be done.
But, friend, if ever we make a plantation
God works a miracle—oh, the bright water
Rushing in the ship's side—and, should we live

I see no reason why we should escape
The gaspings of starvation-wasted men.
Oh, let me die!
For that I do expect, and hourly,
And now, poor William King and I do strive
Which of us shall be meat for fishes first,
Though looking for a glorious resurrection.
Pass my weak matter for my head is weak
And I am still your loving friend, R. Cushman."

The half-hysterical words of a frightened man
Who was not meat for the fishes but went home
Scared out of his wits—yet later crossed the seas
(Let's hope in pleasanter weather!), harangued them all,
Got them to sign the conditions they had refused
And scuttled home to a safe death in London.
You need not take each word that he says for gospel
But that was how the adventure seemed to him
And we shall meet others like him.
                                    Yet they sailed.

She was a sturdy ship, with her double-decks,
High-sterned, slow-sailing, chunky, hard to wear out,
Long in the wine-trade, smelling of it still,
And known for that as a "sweet" ship, meaning a healthy one.
They steered her hundred and eighty tons with a whipstaff.
And she'd trudged the seas for years,
Slow, roomy, durable, smelling of salt and wine,
—A housewife of a ship, not a gallant lady,
Who would groan at storms but get through them and get
    home,

Like a housewife plodding, market-basket in hand—
The *Mayflower*—a common name for ships—
With Christopher Jones of Harwich for her master.
—And what he thought of the voyage, heaven knows,
His business being to sail the ship across,
Land his queer passengers somewhere and return home,
But that was his last voyage, though he knew it not,
For he died ten months after getting back to England,
Neither Puritan nor rogue, but the mere seaman
Who had done his seaman's task and gotten his death
And brought his ship home to sail under other captains.
For that is the chance of the sea.
                              And the trudging housewife
Went on with her work, and plodded from port to port
Till she met the end of every laboring ship,
Though we do not know what it was.
                              We only know
They appraised her, later—at least we think it was she—
And valued her at a hundred and sixty pounds,
Including fifteen pounds for a suit of worn sails.

Now she meets Atlantic, and labors in the grey seas.

And, for those aboard,
We think of them all of one stamp, which they were not.
There were a hundred and one of them all told
But only thirty-five from the Leyden church.
The rest were drawn from London and Southampton
And drawn sometimes, as needs must, from the sort of folk
Willing to stake their lives and seven years
Against a possible future and free land.
They did their best at the choosing, no doubt of that.

They chose Miles Standish, the little chimney soon fired,
Who was to be their buckler in the wilderness;
They picked up young John Alden at the last moment,
For he was a cooper and a hopeful youth;
But there were a number, neither saints nor Puritans,
Who grumbled even while they were still on board
At being ruled by the small band of Zion's men
And swore they would have their liberties, once ashore,
For the patent held for Virginia but not New England.
And, hearing them, Zion's leaders thought it well
To draw a compact, binding their own together
In a lawful government for the town to be.
—And that was to be a cornerstone, in time,
Of something they never visioned from first to last.
But they did not know it then. How could they know it?
They were taking emergency measures in an emergency;
They were founding Zion, not the United States.
—And the seed is sown, and it grows in the deep earth,
And from it comes what the sower never dreamed.

Let us count them now, the beginnings of New England.
There were thirty-eight grown men,
From Brewster and Carver, both of them in their fifties,
To young John Alden and the other bachelors,
Eighteen married women, three of them with child,
Twenty boys, eleven girls
(And seven of these were parish waifs from London
Or seem to have been and no one knows why they came,
But five of the seven died ere they were grown),
Nine servants, five men hired for various tasks,
Including two sailors who would stay but a year,

A spaniel dog and a great mastiff bitch.
And that is the roll. You could write the whole roll down
On a single sheet of paper, yes, even the dogs.
—And, when you have written them down, you write New
    England.

So think of them through the sixty-five long days
Of tempest and fair weather, of calm and storm,
They were not yet Pilgrim Fathers in steeple-hats,
Each with an iron jaw and a musketoon,
They were not Pilgrim Mothers, sure of their fame.
They were men and women and children, cramped in a ship,
Bound for an unknown land and wondering.
The godly prayed, the ungodly spat overside,
The sailors jeered now and then at the pious speeches,
The Billington boys behaved like limbs of Satan,
And the three pregnant women walked the decks
Or lay in their cabins, wondering at night
What hour their pains would strike and what would be born.
In fact, there were human beings aboard the *Mayflower*,
Not merely ancestors.
                              And yet there is
An unforced, almost childish sweetness about the whole
—The sweetness they could muster with their rigor,
The honey of the iron, the naïve
Devoted, confident wonder that made them pilgrims.
Were they sick? They staggered up to the decks and the air
And so felt better. Did the tempest break
And the ship's planks strain and leak? They braced the main
    beam
With an iron jackscrew they'd brought, and all was well.

They might long for the bliss of God and groan at His judg-
  ments,
But they brought with them butter and pease and beer
And the scurvy did not strike and the voyage was healthy.
Only one boy died, a servant of Doctor Fuller's,
While the crew lost four or five, and one most profane,
So God must be with them—God must be with them here,
On the sea as on the land, ever-present God,
With His great right hand outstretched like the Winter cloud.
And Elizabeth Hopkins labored and bore her child,
(*The cries in the narrow cabin, the women waiting*)
And they named the son Oceanus and rejoiced
For that was surely a sign of God's mercies, too,
A fine, strong boy and the mother alive and well.
And Susanna White and Mary Allerton
Knew their time was still to come,
And wondered, seeing the child, when it would be.

And so, at last, on the nineteenth of November,
On a clear, crisp morning, at daybreak,
With a slice of old moon still bright in the dawn-sky,
They saw the long dim outline of Cape Cod.

Then Christopher Jones tacked ship and made for the south-
  ward,
For they thought to settle, perhaps, where the Hudson flowed,
If they might reach it, at least in a milder clime,
But they got among white water and tangled shoals,
They got in the broken part of Pollack's Rip,
Where the currents run like a millrace and veer and change,
The bitter water,

134

The graveyard of ships to come.
They knew that they were in danger from the grim
Faces of crew and captain—but they were landsmen.
There were roaring waters. That was all that they knew.
But Christopher Jones and his sailors knew the truth
And he must have wiped his brow when at last, toward
 evening,
He worked the clumsy *Mayflower* into deep water,
Hove to for the night and knew he'd not lost his ship.
He had not done badly, Captain Christopher Jones,
Though you'll find no statue of him in Plymouth Harbor
And to him, no doubt, 'twas a day's work and no more.

And next day, they looked at the land, and it was good,
A fair land, wooded to the brink of the sea,
Washed with blue, biting air and brave in the sun,
A land for God's plantation.
      And suddenly
They were sick of the ship and the ship's smells and the sea.
They had come so far. They were within sight of land,
Not where they had planned—but land—and the look of it!
Earth after long waters, solid peace in the hand.
They were ready for harbor, now.
        And the sixty-seventh
Day out of England, they let go anchor at last
In Provincetown Harbor, just inside Long Point,
And their firewood was spent and they sent a party ashore,
And there, not on Plymouth Rock, was the first landing.
They searched. They found neither person nor habitation.
But the wood they cut for their fire was juniper
And it smelt very sweet and strong.

Look, if you choose, at the large iced wedding-cake
We have built, at great expense, over Plymouth Rock
(Or over a rock that happened to be at Plymouth)
Look at it well, and buy your souvenirs.
But it does not tell the story.

                                 It does not tell
The silent emptiness of the Winter land,
The smell of the juniper—and the breathless wonder
As they splashed ashore for their First Discovery,
For they couldn't wait for the shallop to be mended.
How could they wait? It was dangerous, of course.
But Captain Standish led them—and you can see them,
The sixteen breathless men,
The staid husbands, the sober fathers of families,
Who had been woolcarders and printers, hosiers and tailors,
With sword and musket and corselet, warily treading,
The new, wild shore, where there might be anything.
And, sure enough, they were hardly well on their way
When they saw five red men—and was it five or six?
They were not quite sure—but there were men and a dog—
You couldn't imagine a dog, but he was there.
They all ran away the moment they were seen,
Swift naked figures, their dog pelting after them,
And the English gave pursuit but could not catch up,
But they had seen Indians.
                            And a little later
They came to a flowing spring, "and we sat us down
And drank our first New England water
With as much delight as ever we drank drink."
Wonderful, to drink water in a new land!
To taste the bright, nipping air!

They were bolder now. They went on. They would not be
    stayed.
They found where a house had been, found a ship's kettle,
Found a heap of sand, smoothed over by Somebody,
And dug in the sand, of course.
                        And there they found
A little old basket full of Indian corn,
Real grains of corn, you could hold them in your hand.
They dug farther—and, oh, there was a fine, great, new
    basket!
With thirty-six ears in it, yellow and blue and red,
And they looked at the ears and passed the ears around.
(And the corn was to help to save them from starvation,
But they did not think of that then. They were busy digging.
Have you ever dug in the earth and found something hidden?
Penny or corn or pearl, it is all the same.
It is treasure-trove, it is the gift of the ground.)
And, after all of them had looked at the ears,
They wondered what to do with the things they'd found.

But they took them along, of course. One always does.
You will carry a stone ten miles, if you've found it so,
And tell everyone about it, once you are home.

And that night it rained. But they camped by a great fire.
(In Somebody's house—in the house of the wild wood.)
They were safe to be sure. They had set up a palisade.
They had their muskets.
                And a Sioux war-party
Could and would have quietly cut their throats
In spite of sleepy sentry or barricade

Ere the morning came.
                              But, landing the year they did,
They were ten times more fortunate than they knew
For, the year before, there had been a plague in the land
And the tribes who might have slain them were dead or broken
Except for a scattered few.
                              And, at dawn, next day,
Having slept all night, yea, verily, on the ground,
(And for some, no doubt, the first time they had ever slept so)
These men of streets and children and settled ways,
Went wandering again through Somebody's house
With the pure excitement of boys at their first camp,
For Somebody had been there but wasn't home,
Though they found his traces—two canoas of his
(You wouldn't have thought they were canoas at first,
But they were, for we looked them over)
And a bent-down tree with something queer at the end,
A noose, made of sinew, aye, and cleverly, too.
Somebody had been there.
They gathered around it, staring, pleased to the bone.
'Tis a deer-trap. Aye. Dost not think so, Neighbor Hopkins?
Aye, a deer-trap. Truly! See! And it worketh so!
And William Bradford boldly investigated
And caught himself in it neatly by the leg
And they all agreed 'twas a very pretty device.
A very pretty device for Somebody.
They couldn't leave it. They had to bring it along.
It wouldn't be any use, but they had to bring it.
And when they got back to the ship and their wives greeted
    them,
Heard about all the things that they had to tell

And were shown the corn and the baskets and the deer-trap,
They had the pride of all hunters, from Nimrod on.

————

Humility Lanyard saw them, coming home,
The small, black, distant figures, walking the beach,
And the women dropped their washing and counted quickly,
Counted with the quick dread.
But there were sixteen. It was well. God had spared them all.
—The first of all the endless waitings and countings,
The long, sick waiting, the count of the frontier,
When your eyes try so hard to see what is far and small
And you tell the children, "Yes—it's all right—it's Father."
But you do not look at the children but at the far
Specks in the boat, by the forest's edge, on the hill,
And why does that one walk lame—and that one carry
Something upon his back—fourteen—fifteen—
But I cannot see him—I cannot see him yet—
Yes—he waves his hand.
Till at last you know by the look of the men's shoulders,
Even far away, whether it is good news or bad,
And can make your face as it should be when they come.
For you must not show the fear. It is bad for them
To have their women show fear.

Humility was not to feel that yet
But Katharine Lanyard felt it—and trampled it
Like a weakness under her feet, as she caught her breath
And stared for Matthew—and yes—he was safe—he was there.
"I can see Father," said the boy Elias,
In his clear little nervous voice. "Has he killed Indians?

Frankie Billington says his father will kill them all.
But Frankie's a wicked boy—"
                                        Then there was a queer
Wail of greeting, like a sea-gull's cry,
From the waiting women, the cry they could not keep down,
Not at this first, not now.
                              The men shouted back,
Clearly and strongly, the hunters coming home.
And—
          "Father looks bigger," thought Humility,
"He looks different, there, with his musket. I don't know
     why."

—————

Somebody's house but Somebody wasn't home—
And the women washed and Susanna White bore her child
And they named the child Peregrine, a wanderer.
And the days slipped
Toward Winter while they explored the river-valleys,
Shot geese and ducks, found two round Indian houses
With tools and baskets, deers' feet and eagle-claws
Lying about in them, but no living thing.
—Somebody's house but Somebody had gone—
Found a grave and dug it up, and in the grave
They found the skull of a man with yellow hair,
Bound up in a canvas cloth.
A packneedle and a knife had been buried with him
And near him were the bones of an Indian child.
And they looked at the skull of the sailor, the English skull,
The skull of the unknown man who had come before,
And thought such thoughts as they might.

Now they all had coughs and colds and the weather hardened.
The face of the land was a weather-beaten face.
They must find their refuge and plant.
And, while they were absent on this discovery,
Young Frankie Billington got hold of a musket
And shot it off, as he would, in the great cabin,
Just missing a little barrel of gunpowder
That might have blown him to bits and staved the ship.
It doesn't say what they did to Frankie Billington
But I'd like to have heard the remarks of Captain Jones.

And then, at last, they met Somebody.
                                        It was cold
And the water froze on their heavy clothes like iron,
Wading from boat to shore.
And there was Somebody—ten or twelve of him,
Busy about a black thing on the beach,
But he ran away again as soon as they saw him,
And the black thing was but a dead grampus, after all.
That day they wandered the woods and saw no people
But, when night began to fall, they hasted away,
For the dark woods changed and moved with the evening
    shadows,
Changed, and drew in about them. They weren't afraid
But they were glad to reach the shallop again
And the men they had left in it rejoiced to see them—
Oh, the vast and echoing Winter woods, the strange
Army of shadows that flit and change with the dusk
And the queer cries in the night—are they owls or men?

And next morning, just at dawn,
They were up betimes, the little exploring party,

Some in the shallop, most of them on shore
Breakfasting, and the arms laid down on the beach
Where they would be less trouble to put aboard.
Then they heard the same strange cry they had heard at night.
The man who was furthest away came running and yelling,
"They are men! Indians! Indians!"
And after him, arrows flickered.

                           There was a confused
And crowded moment as they ran for their arms.
Miles Standish had his snaphance with him and fired it.
But the heavy muskets took years to load and prime.
They yelled to the men in the shallop to be on guard
And the men answered, "Well, well" and "Be of good cour-
    age!"
While three of their pieces went off at Somebody's woods
And they heard the shaking Indian yell go up,
"Woath, Woach! Ha! Hach! Woach! Woath!"
And there was Somebody. There he was at last,
A valiant fellow, red as the autumn leaf,
With bow and arrow. He shot three arrows at them
And they stooped and let the arrows pass over their heads,
But their coats on the palisade were stuck with arrows
And Somebody's chief stood three round shots of a musket,
Till, at last, one valiant Pilgrim aimed straight at him
And saw the splinters fly from Somebody's tree,
And, with that, He gave an extraordinary shriek
And away went they all!
                         They followed a quarter mile.
Somebody had dissolved in the woods like mist.
But they gave two loud shouts, all the same, and fired a volley,
Just to show Somebody.

And that was that,
And nobody had been hurt on either side
But they found eighteen arrows, and they were sure
There must have been more.

      And that was the last they saw
For a long time of bewildered Somebody,
Who, if we know ought, was quite as confused as they
Over the whole proceeding.

      So they went on
In the shallop, through a vile day of snow and rain,
Where first the rudder broke and then the mast,
But they found Clarke's Island and rested there for the night,
And, though they were wet and miserable and cold,
I can hear them talking that night about the wild
Encounter with Somebody, and looking gravely
At the arrows tipped with deer-horn and eagle-claws.
They had fought Indians! And they were still alive.

Next day being Sabbath, they rested and caught their breath,
But the next day, they came to Plymouth and found it
  good,
A wide, fair bay, with cornfields and brooks inland,
A fitting place for Zion.

      So they decided
And went back to tell the news. But, when they returned,
The women looked strange.

      There had been a tragedy
And Bradford's young wife, Dorothy, was dead,
Drowned in the harbor waters.

      We shall not know
How it happened or why it happened or what it was,

143

Chance, loneliness or fate,
That drew her over the side of the *Mayflower*
Into the freezing water, but so she died.
And William Bradford the farm-boy, the self-taught scholar,
Versed in Hebrew and Greek and the hearts of men,
(For he was to rule the colony many years)
Though he writes of other things, writes nothing of this.
For some things cannot be written. Not with a pen.

—They were all alone as few we know are alone.
They made a small, bustling noise in an empty land
But there were times when their voices seemed faint to
    them
Against the enormous stillness, the beast-tracked forest,
The little, careless, slapping sound of the waves
Against the *Mayflower's* side, and the east wind whining.
They could labor and strive but the silence still was silence.
The ship to succor them would not sail for months.
The cold stars above them were as near as England.
They might all die, every one.
Die, and the *Mayflower* rot at her anchorage
And the sea-birds walk on her decks, and the crabs scuttle
And still, for many months, it would not be known.
That was what they faced. That was what they knew might
    be.
That was the question by silence and the loneliness.
Listen. Listen at night. And if you hear any sound,
I do not care how little but any sound
That is not your own breathing,
If you look from your window and see any light not yours,
You cannot even approach their loneliness.

So, at last, they got the *Mayflower* to Plymouth,
And Mary Allerton labored and bore her child,
But it was a son, stillborn.

There is no time to grieve now, there is no time.
There is only time for the labor in the cold,
As we build the city of Zion, in the cold.
As we cast the lots for the houses, plan the street,
On the hill's slope, where the Indian cornfield grew,
For there, God be thanked, is cleared ground.
                              And, a furlong away,
There is still the forest, there is the endless forest,
And we build, and as we build,
We stand between forest and sea as between two paws.

Now tell the tale of the second torment,
Not by fever and heat but by wind and frost,
The slow long torment of the northern god,
The god of the Norther and the knife of stone,
The god with the gull's beak, dipping it in their hearts.

He gave them an open Winter, as if in bounty,
But it was not enough.
                    They were tradesmen and husbandmen,
Shoemakers, weavers, printers, a few servants,
They were strong enough and most were used to hard fare
But, till the voyage, they had been living in towns,
And now they began to die.
                         There was the fierce
New climate, the scanty food and the great toil
And the sickness came—not the fever of the marsh,

But scurvy at last and the sicknesses of the cold,
Striking impartially on ship and shore
Through the bleak first months of the New England year
When the new year lies and wails like a weakling child
In the cold cave, the dark cave, the cave of January,
And you cannot believe the earth will ever grow warm
Or the brooks run out to the sunlight.
                                        It was a grim
Business of backbreak labor in whirling snow
In the gusty, heart-chilling rain. They could faint and die
But the wood must be cut and gathered, the fire kept lit,
And there was the time when their common house caught fire.
The flame did not reach the powder, for God was with them.
And the time two men, John Goodman and Peter Browne,
Went cutting thatch in the forest and spied a deer,
They had the mastiff with them and they gave chase,
Without thought, as hungry men will—you can see them run-
        ning,
You can see them running deeper into the wood,
And stopping then, and whistling the mastiff back,
For the trees had changed and they did not know where they
        were.
They did not know where they were.

And all afternoon they wandered the forest, lost,
Hopeful at first, then doubting.
                                I do not know
Which one of them first saw snow on the back of his hand
And looked at it and knew that it might be death,
For the night fell with the snow, the deep, forest night.
They huddled with the mastiff under a tree,

Gripping the dog by the collar, for through the night,
They heard three lions roaring, three hungry lions,
And the mastiff whined and wanted to go to them.
—And, six months before, John Goodman had been in Ley-
    den,
He must have remembered that with every bone,
As the mastiff strained and his cold fingers slipped
On her heavy collar, and he counted the roarings,
Wondering, numbly, if lions could climb trees.
They had to cut the boots from his swollen feet
When the three of them stumbled into Plymouth at last,
Some twenty-four hours later, stiff and aching.
But there was a stubborn metal in John Goodman.
Only eight days later he went again to the woods,
This time—he would not learn—with a smaller dog.
You could walk with a dog in Leyden, so why not here?
And, all of a sudden, it ran back to him yelping,
With two grey wolves behind it.
                              He threw a stick at them
But they paid not the slightest attention to the stick.
Instead, they sat down on their tails and grinned at him.
They sat there, grinning at him, for some while.

And that, alas, is all we know of John Goodman,
For he was to die of the sickness ere the Spring,
Having heard the roarings of lions that were not there
And faced the wolves that were, and thrown his stick at
    them,
—I can see him, with his dog, in a Leyden street,
Patiently waiting while it lifted its leg
For John Goodman must have liked dogs.

147

                                        He should not have died.
Now the winter hardens, the bitter time begins . . .

                        ————————

They dug the grave for the child on the freezing hill,
The strong child, Martin, the likely, the one to live,
Sure to live. The clods rang under the spade.
He had lived through the worst and died within two days,
Died with the Spring so near, died three years old,
And Matthew Lanyard saw that the grave was deep,
Deep and well-cut, and thought with weary pain,
"I have dug a grave for my son by the wall of Zion
And he sleeps there till the day of the meeting of friends.
Sleeps safe, sleeps sound, will cry no more with the cold.
I do not rebel, my God, though I loved the child.
Yet, O God, look down on our graves, for they are new."

He thought of the child, Devoted, left in England.
She had loved the little brother, and when she came,
She would ask for him as a child asks, merrily.
It was hard to think of that, yet it must be thought of.

By evening the grave was filled and he slept exhausted
But Katharine Lanyard waked and turned at his side,
Still feeling the shape of Martin in her arms.
"I shall bear anew but not Martin, never Martin,
And Rose's daughter lives but my son lies dead.
I am a woman. I may not question God.
But I shall not forget till the end of time."
Then she too slept.
                        And, when the boy Elias
                        148

Moaned in his sleep, for he was afraid to die
And so dreamt much of it, she did not hear him
But Humility did and roused the boy from his dream.
"Hush, 'Lias—you'll wake the others—go back to sleep—"

"I was praying," he said, in his stiff, unchildlike way,
"And the worms destroyed my body but not my soul.
You should not have waked me, sister."

                          "Hush, Elias.
We are all sad, now, but we will pray in the morning
And now you must sleep."

            "The worms will destroy you," he muttered,
Yawned, boyishly, and sank back in the bed again.
She listened a moment until he breathed quietly
Then she tried to think with her mind of the small, good place
But it was hard to find, now, and far away.
The feathering snow whirled over it, with a sound.

———

Write it on iron,
Write it on iron and New England rock,
The story of those four months when they built the town,
For they built it with the dying and the dead.
They built it upon the bones of fourteen women
Who had come for life, not death.
They built it upon the bones of the friends they knew.

And her husband lived but Rose Standish was to die,
A pretty name, Rose Standish, a pretty name,
And her bold little man went nursing sick and dying
With patient and fiery care all Winter through,
Though he had not been a Puritan,

Cleansing the filth of sickness, tending the fires,
Cooking and sweeping, making them eat and drink
And breathing his own quick stubborn life in them
And yet could not save his Rose.
For, when it was worst, but seven of them stayed sound,
The iron Brewster, Miles Standish, and five others,
And the beds were as close together as they would lie
In the common house, the first house they managed to build,
And aboard the ship, the lost seamen cursed and railed,
For they, too, sickened—
                              And one lay cursing his wife,
"Aye, you've driven me here, you bitch, and here I lie."
And another begged his comrade to tend him well,
Promising all he had
For a few days' nursing and a mess of cooked meat
But he lived too long and the comrade called him a cheat
Who would not die when he promised—and yet he died.
Till at last, the dying bosun cried out to Bradford,
"You show your love like Christians, one to another,
But we let one another lie and die like dogs."
—Which doesn't sound much like a bosun, but let it pass.
They were sailors, not men of Zion, and they had come
Not to worship God but because they had signed ship's
    articles,
And yet, a half of them died.
                              And, when it was done,
There were four living women out of eighteen,
The colony cut in half, four households wiped out,
Wife, husband, child and servant, four spared completely.
(And one was the Billingtons and one the Brewsters,
So read that fate as you will.)

And, of the rest,
There were nearly as many children alive as men,
Though some were orphans, now,
But the women, dead and living, had saved the children,
Saved all but six, saved Peregrine, born in the land,
Saved the child born on the sea and named Oceanus
And Samuel Fuller who was but a sucking child,
And the pitiful, tiny clump of houses stood
Where the Indian corn had grown,
And the Winter broke and they looked at each other's faces,
Remembering their dead,
And the birds sang very sweetly, that cold Spring.

———

It is done. The dice have been cast,
The wave has gone west at last
That will turn back no more,
Against the painted year.
There are houses standing here
That were not standing before.

Now the long, crooked coast lies open, now the fishermen find
    the Banks.

A handful here and a handful,
A scrabble of hard-won ground
And nothing sure that they know.
The South and the North are begun,
The green corn blooms in the sun,
The clearings grow.

Now New France grows and New Netherland begins, now the priests land in the North, now the Dutchmen trade by the Hudson. Now it is a year and a year since the burgesses met at Jamestown in the summer-hot church, twenty-two men discussing small matters, and yet not to be forgotten, for they speak for themselves and try to rule themselves and that will not be forgotten. (And the same year the first slaves are bought and that will not be forgotten also.)

And oddly and by chance,
By the working circumstance,
By the hard extremity,
By loneliness and need,
By frost and fever-sweat,
And the rebellious mind,
By all they have given up,
By all they have come to find,
They carry the sleeping seed
That will not waken yet,
The small seed, liberty.

———

Jack of the Feather's out again,
That savage, bold and sly,
He passed, he passed by Morgan's house
And so did Morgan die.

He took poor Morgan into the wood
And there he made him bleed.
Then he came back to Morgan's house
Not three days after the deed.

The boys who dwelt at Morgan's house
Beheld him in his pride,
"The savage wears our master's cap,
But where does Master bide?

"The villain wears our master's cap
And it is stained with red.
Now Jack of the Feather shall not live
With that cap upon his head."

They primed their pieces handily,
They talked with him awhile
And they shot Jack of the Feather down
Ere he had gone a mile.

Yet, ere he died, he said a word
And it was grimly said,
"My chieftain loved me while I lived.
He'll prize me when I'm dead.

"He is not sleepy Powhatan
To bluster and forget.
My chieftain, Ophechancanough,
Who will avenge me yet."

It was only a few days afterwards,
It was on Good Friday morn,
That the savages to our houses came
With fish and fruit and corn.

The savages to our houses came
As friend goes in to friend.
We thought they came in peace and trade
But that was not their end.

For, hardly had they entered in
(And some of us still at meat)
When they began the bloody work
That is not yet complete.

They sat and broke their fast with us
And then they rose with a shout
—And then you could hear the women scream
As the English blood ran out.

They fell upon us in the field
And by the cradle-head,
And they were lucky who died the first,
For they were quickly dead.

They fired Lieutenant Basse's house.
They burned at Flowerdieu.
And Captain Berkeley and all his folk
They barbarously slew.

At Master Macock's Divident
They slew but only four,
But at the college we'd begun,
They slew almost a score.

Alas for Martin's Hundred
Where seventy-three lie slain,
Alas for the six counselors
We shall not see again!

Alas, alas, for Powell's Brook,
'Tis bloody water there,
And, where the kindly houses stood
The haggled corpses stare.

Yet Master Baldwin beat them off
And Captain Hamer, too,
And Mistress Proctor would not flee
For all that they might do.

A civil and modest dame she was
As ever squeaked at a mouse,
But she kept her house like a musketeer
Till the rescue came to her house.

A modest and gentle dame she was
As ever sewed on a clout,
But she would not leave her lovesome house
Till the soldiers forced her out.

God's blessing on the providence
That made one heathen hark
And so betrayed the deadly plot
Ere all of us lay stark.

God's blessing on the providence
That moved that heart of brass,
God's curse on Ophechancanough
That brought the thing to pass.

And now we plant the corn again
And reckon up the score.
Three hundred forty-seven dead
From the forest to the shore.

And now we plant the corn again
But, when the harvest's due,
We'll see that Ophechancanough
Shall have a harvest, too.

We'll reap among his heathen fields
With musket and with gun,
And there'll be little left to glean
When that red reaping's done.

Three hundred forty-seven dead.
They shall not lie alone
When we meet with Ophechancanough
And reap what he has sown.

———————

Dickon Heron, the night before,
Dreamt that he ran by the Devon shore
A child who tugged at his mother's hand
And skipped white pebbles along the strand
While his mother's voice came low and soft,
Sleepy as wind in a pigeon-loft

"Liddle Dickon, look in thy hand,
Sudden journey and sudden dole,
Mind 'ee of that in the foreign land,
Liddle sparrow, Dickon, my soul."
Then he tired of the pebbles though they were fair
And her hand came smoothing his ruffled hair
As they both looked seaward and saw the breaker
Stride toward the beach for the land to take her
And in it the sea-thing, cold and brave,
That swam with the wave and was of the wave,
Child of its thunder and its speed,
White-armed, crowned with a wreath of weed
And staring with bright, immortal eyes
At the land-born flesh that lives and dies,
Staring a moment and then sunk down
To the long green glimmer of Merman's Town,
The town of the sunken glooms and gleams
Where the fish go swimming through drowned men's dreams;
"Aye, 'tis the Swimmer," his mother said,
And he knew by her voice that they both were dead
And the dream dissolved—and Sir Gilbert Hay
Sat, picking his teeth, on a mound of clay
And smiling his tight-lipped gamester's smile
Till the jaw dropped slowly, after a while,
And the eyes were frozen in the head
And the dream dissolved—and Dickon sped
Through an endless wood on an endless quest,
West and west and forever west,
And with him traveled a faint, thin crying
That was something living and something dying,
A cry like an arrow, a fateful cry

Of the flesh that knows mortality
And yet will run while the heart can beat
Though it goes at last upon stumbling feet,
Till, at length, it ceased, and there was no sound
And Dickon caught breath and looked around.
There was nought behind and nought before
But the green, Spring leaf and the forest floor
And the squirrel chirked in the sycamore
As if it had never heard of man
But the blaze on the tree read "Croatan".
The word of peril, the lost men's word.
And the dream dissolved—and Dickon stirred,
Stirred and roused and thought with a yawn
"That must be the wind before the dawn
And I shouldn't have supped on herring-roes
For a man's no business with dreams like those.
I shan't tell Alice—she'd half believe,
For she loves the tales of Midsummer Eve,
But, as for walking the shores of Devon,
I'll never do that this side of heaven,
And Mother, God rest her! dead six years—
And yet, it was strange, for I saw her tears.
Now, what did she say? Nay, I forget.
But I felt her tears and the tears were wet.
And they lost their lives at Croatan
But that was long before we began
And things are different at Heron's Bend.
Aye, you've not done badly, Dickon, my friend.
For you might have starved and you might have hung
And, if you had stayed in London town,
You might have married a nagging tongue,

Fattened your haunches and settled down
With a 'What d'ye lack?' and a 'Tenpence each'
And a 'Pray will your worship come kick my breech?'
A pursy cit with a long-nosed daughter
Who feeds his prentices beans and water,
Snug as a bug in his chimney-corner
And proud of it all as Little Jack Horner
For he hopes—Good God!—at the end of labor
To have an alderman call him neighbor!

I have given no pledge, I have made no vow,
But they call me Captain Heron now
And this is a world where a man starts clear
Once he's paid the price of getting here,
For, though we be English, true and staunch,
We'll judge no man by the size of his paunch
And my lord's lackey and my lord's station
Have little to do with a man's plantation,
For here is a knight and a Newgate debtor
And which of the two will prove the better?
Can you read the riddle? I will not try
But we live under another sky
From the men who never have crossed the seas
And the fleas that vex us are other fleas.
For I thought I came for a lump of gold
But I shall die like a squire of land
With my sons about me, hardy and bold,
And something grown that I never planned.
Heron's Bend, Heron's Bend,
Sons to foster and fields to tend,
And we shall prosper, before the end."

He was down in the fields when the Indians came,
Led by Johnny, the fat and tame,
The thieving fellow that all knew well
For the rogue had always something to sell,
"Werowance" Johnny, so called in sport,
For, when he was drunk he would puff and snort
And call himself son of Powhatan,
"Me brave Johnny—me valiant man!"
Harmless Johnny, scorned by his nation,
Who made the rounds of each out-plantation
To beg what he might, steal what he could,
And then, like smoke, drift back to the wood,
Dressed in his tatters of English gear
With a copper button stuck in his ear,
A broken hat on his greasy hair
And the look of a tamed and greedy bear.
"Aye," thought Dickon, with some vexation,
"And I would he had chosen the next plantation,
For the fellows with him have hatchets, too,
And they'll eat like horses. They always do.
Waste a day's work with their heathen chatter
And scare the new girl just by looking at her.
Well, I'd better see that they get no liquor.
There's nought makes a savage a devil quicker
And Johnny can smell it, hot or cold."

He called to Tommy, his seven-year-old.
"Son, run up to the house and say
We've visitors from the woods today
And they'd better put the liquor away.
Your mother knows."

"But it's Johnny, dad!
Can't I stay and see him? I won't be bad
And he said, next time, he'd make me a bow."

"Later, sonny."

    He watched him go,
Scudding along like a rabbit-child
With his small legs pumping, his hair blown wild,
Thinking, "Now why are my hands asweat?
He'll be safe at the house and there's nothing yet.
It's been years and years since the peace was sealed
But—we've no muskets, here in the field—
And I like not the look of that tallest joker.
He's painted his face with soot and ocher,
Painted for war—and they're spreading out—
Ah, would, would you?" He gave a shout
"Run, Tom, run!"—for, over his head,
The unbelievable arrow sped
And he heard a shriek from the drying-shed.

There were four men there and five in the field
And life hung on seconds. He roared and wheeled.
"Up, lads, up, with shovel and hoe!
We'll teach the rascals to treat us so!
If they get to the house, the women are done,
But they'll break if we rush them. On, set on!
Will you squat and die like pigs at a fair?"

He saw them straighten. He saw them stare.
But the painted men were everywhere.
He struck at one with a shaven crown

And the spade bit deep and the man went down
But then he was wrestling, foot to foot,
With a fellow who stank of grease and soot
But made no sound as he lunged and strove,
Though he glared at Dickon as if with love
As they stamped and trampled the wet Spring sod,
"Strong," thought Dickon, "too strong, by God!
Alice, I taught you to prime the piece!"
Then his fingers slipped on the body-grease
And the hatchet rose and he saw it fall
But felt no hurt of the blow at all,
For there were the shots. He could hear them plain
As the hatchet rose and fell again.

Then he woke for a moment, or so it seemed,
Though he could not tell if he woke or dreamed,
For someone was carrying someone hurt
And his legs or theirs were trailing the dirt,
And then it was Alice's face awhile
Though he was vexed that she would not smile,
"The boat," he whispered; "get to the boat,
If there's enough of her left to float,
Get downriver—get to the town.
I'd walk if I could, but I fall down."

And her voice came murmuring, low and soft,
Like the noise of Spring in a pigeon-loft
But he could not hear her. He cocked his head.
" 'Tis a niggling thing, to die," he said,
With one last look of his sparrow's eye
At the darkness rushing from earth and sky,

"But we've done what never men did before
And Tom and Jack will settle the score.
Kiss me, Alice—I'm going fast.
Yet the luck's been ours, and the luck will last,
And how he'll goggle, good Master Knapp,
When I show him the fortune in my cap!"
Then the whisper ceased, for the tale was told,
And the hand she touched was heavy and cold.

Alice Heron rose up, dry-eyed
And turned to the folk who stood beside,
And all that she saw was deadly clear
As she strove for the words that would make them hear,
The white-faced women, the wounded men,
The room that smelt like a slaughter-pen,
The clock still ticking against the wall
And the silent children, watching all.
"He is dead," she said, "but I was his wife
And 'tis nine miles down to the fort and life
And we must do it ere set of sun
For they'll strike again when the night's begun.
But I'd carry him there on my own bent back
Ere I left him here for these wolves to hack.
Have you heart to follow? You must and will.
For my kerchief's wet with his lifeblood still
And they hewed him down in his own plowed field.
Now see what weapons your hands can wield."

It was so she got them, stricken and spent,
To the shallop moored where the river bent
And there lay Johhny, the fat and sly,

Crawled to the edge of the stream to die
With his face in the water and his long hair
Stirring like snakes in the ripple there.
She looked for a moment and turned away.
"Now, that's well," she murmured. "That's well, I say."
And her skirts brushed over the stiffened hand
As they got the shallop in close to land.
They could hasten, now. There was life to find
And only the children looked behind
As they filled the boat with living and dead,
And, when that was done, "Cast off!" she said,
Knowing her sorrow, "Nay, little Jack,
We go for a while but we will come back.
They shall not root us from what we've won,
Aye, but hold me tightly, Tommy, my son."
For now, as the shallop put from shore,
There were slipping shapes in the fields once more,
And they saw the flicker of flame ascend
And the fires begin at Heron's Bend.

————

And the years pass by and are gone, the years pass by
And we may not tell of them all.
                              If this song is
Crooked as rivers, rough as the mountain-range
And many-tongued and a wanderer to the end,
It must be so, for it follows the giant land,
It follows the ways and the roads and the wanderings,
Not one man's fate.
                    O forest of a land,
With your broad continents of night and day,

Sea of a land, endless and asking land,
How may we begin to know you with any song,
How may we say one word and utter your name?

Yet listen, now, to the small and human voices,
To the first and stammering voices of the men
Who cling like wasps to the rim of the continent,
As a climber clings to a cliff, to the men and women
Who make the first fires against darkness, against the cold,
And the fires shall not be put out.

                    Humility Lanyard
Walked home with the others, one Sabbath of early Spring,
And knew that her heart was changed and the world was new,
Although there was nothing yet and the Spring was late,
But, if you ruffled the old leaves under your hand
There was arbutus beneath them, and it bloomed.
And Henry Shenton, come in the *Paragon*,
The butcher's son with the white impassioned face
Who had lain in the straw of jails and found it sweet,
For there one might think and suffer and yet find God,
Felt something stir in him that he had never known.
He had listened most attentively to the prayers
And noted eight points of godly disputation
Which, being gentle, he would not argue yet
But rather love these men for the faith they had,
Yet now he forgot them, thinking of a girl's face.

And the years pass, the priceless years,
With the small proud tale, the tale of harvest and drouth,
The small events that are mighty, the corn, the fish,

The green tobacco growing over Virginia,
The Indian stayed, the new folk coming across,
To plant here and there, to fail, to starve as the first,
Yet ever there are more.
There is Samuel Maverick at Noddle's Island.
There is John Brown, at Pemaquid.
                                    There are
A dozen, a score, a troop, who plant and fail,
Plant and succeed, and die in the land but plant.
And here comes Thomas Morton of Clifford's Inn,
Gentleman, sportsman, lawyer, ironist,
The one man with a sense of humor in all New England.
The man who tried to set Merry England up
With its routs and maypoles on bare New England earth,
And he came too late and Merry England was sped,
And they hewed his maypole down and they caught him
     drunk,
Jailed him, expelled him, ruined his Merry Mount,
They hoisted him, bound and protesting, aboard a ship
And sent him home—and yet the man would return,
For again, as it was with Smith, he loved the country.
He drank the country down like a cup of sack,
This laughing man who had come to it at forty,
Treated his Indians as living men
Not as heathens sure of the pit unless they prayed
And sold them guns and powder without a care.
(And that was a stark matter of life and death
For the guns were the white man's power and his secret.
The motive's mixed but the mathematics are plain.)
Oh, it's easy to see why they hated you, Thomas Morton,
And yet, they would have hated without the guns.

It was the tongue in your cheek that they hated most,
The last flare of Old England, the reckless mirth.
They silenced much, but that tongue they could not silence
And you died at last, old and crazy, at York in Maine.
Or they say old and crazy. I do not know.
Humorists do, sometimes, but I do not think so.
I think you drank your cup of wine to the lees
And chuckled, dying, thinking of Captain Shrimp.

More dubious men,
Christopher Gardiner, Knight of the Holy Sepulchre,
Who left two wives in London but brought a mistress,
Was nobly entertained for being a knight,
Made trouble, ran off to the woods, stole a warming-pan,
Went back to England and there made trouble anew.
(They are coming, now, the crackbrained and the sound,
The oddities, the enthusiasts, the daring,
Some for God and some for the swimming fish,
They are spirited to Virginia in the ships,
Kidnaped, some, for the head-right, but they come.)

And there is another house at Heron's Bend
And the stones of the hearth know fire and Dickon's sons
Roam in the wood, tall boys with gipsy eyes.
There is Jemmy Crews and he sits in their father's place,
For a woman must wed, and he is a steady man,
And they like him well but he will not be their father,
And Alice Crews, who was Alice Heron, sings:

"Living and dead
And the white cloud overhead

And the grass new.
The child, born for the care,
The breast to give it there,
These things are true.

I was young. I knew the sweet.
It shook me from head to feet.
I'll not deny it.
Yet, even when that's gone,
There's something must live on
And I live by it.

I will plant posies still,
Knowing he loved them well
And me, his creature.
Yet give another man
Such bounty as I can,
For that's my nature.

The nature that is made
Not choice of sun or shade,
Nor wanton nor afraid
But earth's true lover.
That lives, like sky and grass,
That lives and will not pass,
That shares the thing it has
Over and over.

And, when I'm old and blind
And death comes with the wind
And flesh of mine must find

Long refuge for him,
My body I'll prepare.
Yet life first sojourned there,
The strong son, hard to bear
And yet I bore him."

———————

Matthew Lanyard strode through the summer dusk,
Knowing his God was with him and most just
Though it had been a grim and heart-searching day.
There was nothing strange to him now in land or skies.
This was Zion. The first rude cabins were half-forgot.
There was meeting house and blockhouse and the long street.
They had planted the corn for ten years and it was good corn.
They had lasted out many things.
                          They had lasted out
Plague, famine, threats from the red men and Mr. Weston
And it was a long time now since Squanto came
And showed them how to plant the fish with the corn,
A long time since the first wonder and the first fear.

He did not think of these things but his body knew them.
You would not come up behind him in the wood
Without his hearing you, now, and when he looked
At sky or sea, it was with the testing eyes
Of the man who knows the weather under his skin,
The man who smells the weather in the changed breeze
And has tried himself against it and lived by it.
It is a taut look but there is a freedom in it.

He thought, "And now they come, after long last,
The new men, the new ships, and it is well.

A thousand, they say—a thousand in the ships,
And we were but a hundred when we came
And they'll bring goods and cattle—settle near—
And I wish them well, good men, and yet a thousand!
'Tis hard to think of, for it seemed, at times,
As there were not a thousand living men
Left in the world, but only wolves and heathen,
And we, we banded few, who starved and bore,
And yet have done the thing and there it stands.

A thousand. They must come. Of course they must.
They are our brothers. Yet we were the first
And Kate will wonder if they're truly saved,
For that she ever does. 'Tis hard to rede,
She would drive forth where I would not drive forth
And I can see her in my growing sons
And yet, we came in love. Let that be said.
We came in passionate and friendly love
With God before us like a walking cloud.

No—no—not all—not every one of us—
I know that, too—but there was something then,
Aye, in that first most sad and stricken year,
Even in the starvation, which is gone.
We're safer, surer and more prosperous,
We have set up a candle for the world.
We have built Zion. Aye, but have we built?

Cometh John Endicott, a worthy man
But harsher than our folk, though full of God.
Come now these others—aye—and after them

How many and how many through the years?
A troop, a multitude, a swarming host,
And what will they be building?
                                    I'd not say
This to another man and least to Kate,
Only to thee, only to thee, my God,
Who knowest the dark fabric of the heart,
The sin, the soilure and the mortal ill
And still, unflinchingly, dost judge us all.

I think we harden somewhat in our hearts
And look, perhaps, too close on one another,
Searching too swiftly for a neighbor's fault
In the cold Winters when the dark comes soon,
For thou art sun and light as well, my God.
There I have said it. Only Thou didst hear.

I was an idle lad and am God's man.
I have endured much and will more endure.
We have built Zion in the wilderness.

O sons, remember we were small and few
And yet God carried us across the seas
And we were loving, and we built the town
And clenched each nail that's in it with our hearts."

Now he passed by the gallows-foot and the thing dangling
And something dark, beneath it, gave eldritch tongue.
"Good Master Lanyard, when will ye take him down?"
He stopped with a shudder for he had not seen her
But he knew the voice, he could not forget the voice,
And his mind went back more years than he cared to count

To a room and the smell of birth and a newborn child
Held in the hands that now were old woman's claws.
"Good Master Lanyard,
D'ye know there's a new little Puritan in the world?"

"Joan Billington," he said, "go back to your house."
"My house?" said the voice. "Aye, I had hearth and house.
I had a son and ye've strung him up on a rope
And 'a dangles there like a mawkin—poor, pretty Jack,
With his neck as long as a goose's neck, poor lad!
And yet, I'll keep him company, Master Lanyard."
She chuckled once and horribly. "Aye," she said,
" 'Tis Jack's old mother must aye keep him company.
You'll not change that with your praying, so pray away!"

"Woman," he said, "your son was a murtherer.
The blood was proved upon him in open court."

Then he stopped, for it was no use.
                              "Aye, sirs," she said,
"They tell us we'll all be rich and free in the land.
But they've hanged my Jacky."
                              He tried to lay his hand
Upon her but his own flesh shrank at the touch.
"Joan Billington," he said, "go home to your house.
We will pray for you. We did not do this in haste.
We have no hardness against you in our hearts."

She chuckled again and looked at him cunningly.
"Aye," she said, "but the crows will pyke at his eyes.
They'll be fine, fat bits for the crows, so I must bide.
Master Lanyard, when will ye cut him down?"

"Tomorrow, woman," he said and turned away.
He must not hurry, being a man, and did not,
But he could hear her terrible voice in his ears.
"D'ye hear that, Jacky? Tomorrow you'll be cut down.
You'll be home tomorrow, lad—aye, be patient now.
For your old mother is waiting. She'll scare the crows.
She'll keep the crows from your face, poor Jacky boy,
And a pretty face it was and I gave it suck—
Adear, adear—and how it tugged at the teat!
But that was in Merry England, long ago,
And Merry England's gone, all spent and gone."

He wiped his brow and breathed in the sweet night air.
He would not force the woman against her will.
—They had always been a nuisance, the Billingtons,
A brawling, turbulent family—and now this—
For the man had slain John Newcomen in cold blood
And it was proved—and yet he could hear her voice,
Babbling on, half-crazed, the human voice
That Elias, for all his piety, seldom had.
Did she think it was so easy to hang a man?
A man who came with the first and should have thriven?
He tried to pray.
The words would not come, at first, and then they came.
"And yet, I know we came in love," he said.

————————

"It is well," thought Katharine Lanyard, "I have done well,"
As she stooped and rose and stooped in her garden-plot,
The hard, firm garden that grew like her own will.
There was pain, these days, but she could master the pain.

It was only in the body, the despised
Shortsighted body, the fool that changed with the years,
The renegade that fought one so stubbornly,
First with love and now, as it seemed, with pain.
"Aye, I have done well," she thought, with her own passion,
"I have sealed my seed for God and they will not change.
It is the reward of the just.
                              And the woman came
With her lewd, old, slubbered face, came asking an alms,
And the bread I gave her she ate with her bitter tears,
In her tears she ate it, the woman who called me barren
When she had lusty children and I had none,
And it was meet she should eat her bread in the dust.
They should have hanged the woman beside her son.
We must root all wickedness out. We have but begun."

She thought of the boy Elias, the boy grown man,
With a deep sure pleasure. He was flesh of her flesh,
Bone of her bone and turning to her always.
"Aye, Matthew does not know him, but I know.
He has seen the wickedness in this Henry Shenton,
The deadly wickedness under the godly cloak,
And he will be a burning and shining light.
I shall hear them groan and quake when he speaks the Word,
I shall see him drive the ungodly with whips of cords.
And the others follow after, the younger ones,
There is not one of them unacquainted with wrath
And none shall be a scorner—and yet, I fear.
For the new days come and new folk who are not as we.
We must bind our bonds with iron to keep all fast.
Yet it will be done. Have I served You well, my God?

I think I know in my heart we have served You well
And to the uttermost farthing of the bond."

So she thought and crushed the cutworm upon the leaf
For it ate what it should not eat and it knew not God
And so she would do to any who knew not God.
—And the whippings and the hangings were yet to come,
Yet to come, in New England,
The blood of the Quakers, crying out from the ground,
The witch hunts, the iron rigor, the age of ice—
But she rejoiced in her ways, for her ways were righteous,
And her son, Elias, would follow them, after her.

————

Humility sat and sewed by her husband's side.
—Henry Shenton, come in the *Paragon*,
The butcher's lad with the white, impassioned face,
Older now but still with the mark on him
That shows the seeker, the man who is not content.
The babes were asleep but her husband was by her side
And he turned the leaves of a book, but she was content.
"Frail love, arbutus of the cold, bare Spring.
We have found you in the wood and it is enough
For I knew that the word was love, not fear or pain,
And I must not vex him with that for he thinks of God,
Yet I know that the word was love."
                              He put down the book.
"Wife," he said, "when they come—the new colony—
And it seems they must—the men who come to the Bay—
Would it grieve you to leave this house?"
                              "Aye, husband," she said,

Remembering deep in her youth and the small, good place
And a father and mother talking while she listened,
Talking of voyages that were so far,
"Aye, it would grieve me somewhat, for the babes are young.
But if we must go, we must go."
                                        He ruffled his hair
In the one small boyish gesture that she loved.
"They are good men, here," he said in a solemn voice,
"And yet it is laid upon me to seek new ways.
I have kept my peace since we two were wed, Humility,
And yet I am not content on some points of grace.
I am not content. I have labored with Master Bradford
And he is full of the very spirit of God—
And yet, meseems, that he erreth; though, in the Hebrew,
It is also written—"
                                Her mouth and her face were grave
But she longed to say, "Dear heart, do I not know?
Dear heart that was kept in prison and fought the world
And so must ever seek for a thing unfound
And will not yield to the world, and yet is sweet.
You need not look so solemnly with your eyes,
For, without your eyes, I would know that we two must go.
And I am not strong as certain women are strong,
Yet I can bear more than they."
                                    "They'll have books," he said,
"And I deem we may have much profitable discourse.
Nor may the things in my heart be always hid.
Have we fled England to live here under a rule,
And a dry rule, too—a dead and formal staff?
Nay, I'd speak of it to no other—but thou knowest—
The spirit works upon me and I must go."

"We will go," she said. "Now, am I not dutiful?"
And he stared at her for a moment and then he smiled
And, when he did, the face was boyish enough.
"Did I ever tell thee?" he said.
                              "The butcher's boy!
Go tell!"
              "But I have told it so often, wife."
"Nay, tell!"
              "Well, there was a butcher's boy, it seems.
And a profane swearer."
                          "Was he?"
                                      "Aye, I could tell
But I will not."
                  "Oh, the horrible, cursing oaths!
Dost thou really know them?"
                              "Aye, and a dozen more
For then was I unregenerate and a child."

"I can see thee unregenerate, yet go on."

"Well, this butcher's boy would bully the smaller lads,
For he had a great, strong fist like a sheep's quarter,
And there was one—"
                      "Aye, thou!"
                                    "—Who was unregenerate,
And yet had some small stirrings within his heart
For he loved his book, aye, even the books of stage-plays—"

"I can see thee, reading!"
                          "And it was this butcher boy's
Particular concern to harry this lad,
Who, being small and pale and a coward, fled."

177

"Thou wert no coward!"
                        "Peace, who telleth the tale?
—And, one day, caught him—"
                                "Oh!"—
                                        "In an alley way,
With book in hand and a string of sausages
In t'other he must deliver or be well whipped.
So, seeing his foe, the small pale lad would have run."

"Thou wouldst not."
                        "Aye, but there was but the one way out
And the fellow struck the sausages to the ground,
Though, with much Christian goodwill, the lad prayed him
    nay.
But, when the fellow took the book from his hand
And tore its leaves, though it was a silly book
—The Tale of Robin Hood and yet I loved it—
The small pale lad burst into such tears of wrath
That he fell like David upon that butcher's boy
—Yea, as David upon Goliath, though with no stone—
And did so notably thump and pummel him
(Sheer rage it was—and the Cumberland wrestling trip
He had learned in the market from the unregenerate)
That the big boy went home squalling with two black eyes
And after that, molested the lads no more."

"And what did the small pale lad—?"
                                "Oh, he was whipped
For spoiling the sausages."
                        "Cruel!"
                                "Nay, most just.

Yet, after that, he was not as he was before,
For he did not fear—and why dost thou like the story?"
"I like it. Thou wilt always fight butcher's boys."

"I fear so, wife."
                    "And I love thee for it. So."
She took his hand in hers and stared at the fire
Thinking, "And, since he wishes, then we will go.
I could like content and we will not have content.
But it is best that we go, being what he is."
She saw some sort of future in the fire
But not what was to happen, for she could not.
Salem and Boston and the harried life,
The speaking out—the trial—the warning words—
The face of Katharine Lanyard, bitter and grim,
Drawing aside as Henry passed to the jail,
The second trial, the second driving forth,
The long and terrible journey through winter woods
And the safety in Rhode Island, in the fair,
New-planted place that Roger Williams loved
With its bright weather and its sweet-tongued rain,
Good for all roses and all exiles always,
The new place, where a man might speak his mind;
But all began from the first again for a woman,
Yes, all from the beginning, the naked ground.
But, if she had seen, she'd not have turned aside
For she was Humility and her mother bore her.

And he, the seeker, sitting by her side,
The butcher's son who would never bow to the strong,
The man with the fearful strength of the gentle in him,

The man who would bear all whips and bonds for the truth,
Dreamt of a world where none would be whipped or bound
But all men live like brothers, though not yet.

————

End the song, end the song,
For now the flood goes west, the rushing tide,
The rushing flood of men,
Hundred on hundred, crowding the narrow ships.
Massachusetts begins, and Providence Plantations,
Connecticut begins, Virginia spreads out.
There are Swedes by the Delaware, Scotchmen after Dunbar,
They whip the first Quaker bloodily through the street.
Exile, rebel, men against fortune, all
Who are driven forth, who seek new life and new hope
As the wheel of England turns, they are coming now
To the exile's country, the land beyond the star.
(Remember that till you die. Remember that.
Remember the name of the outcast and the stranger.
Remember that when you say
"I will have none of this exile and this stranger
For his face is not like my face and his speech is strange."
You have denied America with that word
Though your fathers were the first to settle the land.)
A rolling, resistless wave of seeking men,
Settling and planting, creeping along the coast,
Pushing up river-valleys to the new ground,
Winthrop and Hooker and Williams—Father John White
Who prayed to all the angels of the Americas,
(For they must be there) as they settled Maryland.
There was a wind over England and it blew.

There was a wind through the nations, and it blew.
Strong, resistless, the wind of the western star,
The wind from the coasts of hope, from the barely-known,
And, under its blowing, Plymouth and Jamestown sink
To the small, old towns, the towns of the oldest graves,
Notable, remembered, but not the same.
This was where we planted—aye—but the corn has grown,
The corn has grown to a rustling yellow field,
And a trembling hand writes down,
"This year, thirty persons still living of the old stock."
Standish—Brewster—the names fade out with the wind—
The names ring fainter, the names of the first, the bold,
"This year twelve persons still living of the old stock."
They have gotten their children. They sleep in Burial Hill.
They sleep by the Jamestown church. They sleep well and
    long.
Though their seed be increased, they know their seed no more.
This last, this seventieth year,
"Two persons living that came in the first ships"
Of the old stock . . . the old stock . . .
There are two . . . there are none at last . . .
Of the old stock . . . the old stock . . .

And the west wind blew in the faces of Dickon's sons
And they looked to the West and searched it with their eyes,
And there was the endless forest and the sharp star.